T0208723

# RETIREMENT
## REORIENTATION

## Short Stories and Tall Tales

## JACK E. BYNUM

**WESTBOW**
PRESS
A DIVISION OF THOMAS NELSON
& ZONDERVAN

WestBow Press books may be ordered through booksellers or by contacting:
WestBow Press
A Division of Thomas Nelson & Zondervan
1663 Liberty Drive
Bloomington, IN 47403
www.westbowpress.com
1 (866) 928-1240

ISBN: 978-1-4908-4863-1 (sc)
ISBN: 978-1-4908-4862-4 (hc)
ISBN: 978-1-4908-4861-7 (e)
Library of Congress Control Number: 2014914810

Printed in the United States of America.
WestBow Press rev. date: 09/11/2014

**To Margaret**
My companion in these adventures:
Amavimus, Amamus, Amabimus

# ACKNOWLEDGMENTS

The following individuals are saluted for their proportional reviews of the original manuscript of this book and their encouragement and suggestions to the author. Gratitude is also extended to the technical and production advisors listed below for their professional assistance in the completion of this book project.

**Manuscript Reviewers:** Teresa Cortez, Herbert Douglass, Leo Downing, Herbert Ford, George Hilton, Ruben Ramkissoon, and Paul Scott.

**Technical Support:** Robert Connolly: computer guru; Alice Jenkins: publishing consultant; and Dale McAlester: research assistant.

# CONTENTS

# INTRODUCTION

## Going Home

My name is Jack Bynum. My wife, Margaret, and I met over sixty years ago when we were college students in Northern California. After college graduation and marriage, we lived and worked several years in the San Francisco Bay Area before my aspirations for more education led us to the small city of Ashland in Southern Oregon. Margaret Clary was born in Ashland, where her pioneer family still has deep roots. I attended nearby Southern Oregon State University for a year before graduating with a Master's degree in sociology and education. Then we moved on to a four-year doctoral program at Washington State University. After graduating with my doctorate, Margaret and I migrated two thousand miles to the Midwest with our two young children for a long and fulfilling teaching and research career at Oklahoma State University.

We loved Oklahoma and the people in "Cowboy Country"— especially the thousands of outstanding faculty and students at that beautiful university. How much I enjoyed the day-by-day and year-by-year involvement in campus life! I will never forget the overwhelming excitement and challenge of teaching and learning, the athletic subculture with football as a local religion, the nostalgic spirit of Homecoming Weekends, and the inspiring ritual and regalia of graduation ceremonies. The carillon bell tower ringing the traditional "Gaudeamus Igitur" across the campus was a fitting and final memory as I neared the end of my many happy years as a student and teacher *("Let us rejoice while we are young … for tomorrow we are old")*.

I have already shared many details of those experiences with my readers in an earlier book (Bynum 2006). So without lingering on the previous career path of my life, it is time to embark upon the retirement journey and some related experiences and issues encountered by the author and many readers about to vicariously join me through the pages of this book.

## The Transition Begins

One warm and humid evening in 1995, Margaret and I stood in the front yard of our cottage near the university in Stillwater, Oklahoma. An hour earlier we had fled to a storm shelter while another series of seasonal tornados ravaged large portions of Oklahoma and Texas. I must confess: going through an Oklahoma twister can make people more religious. No wonder all those churches (still standing) were packed on Sunday mornings! I recall one storm flattening a long row of parking meters. Heavy, two-inch diameter pipes offer little wind resistance, but there they were—grotesquely twisted over the concrete curb.

After that 1995 storm had moved on to demolish entire neighborhoods in Tulsa, Margaret and I were thankful that only the roof of our Stillwater house was partially missing. We were grateful to have a second home—a nearly new, sturdy brick structure three hundred miles south near Fort Worth, Texas. However, a quick telephone call revealed that another tornado had damaged the roof of that house, and neighbors were clearing the street where two large trees from our yard had fallen. Margaret and I looked at each other and said, "We have reached retirement age. Why are we still here?" The next question focused our need for a decision: "Where shall we go?"

I am not defaming the great state of Oklahoma. On the contrary, the residents are typically friendly, hard working, religious, and patriotic. The Oklahomans are among the bravest people I have ever met—not only those thousands who endured the Dust Bowl tragedy of the 1930s and migrated out to California, but those who remained in Tornado Alley to literally restore the soil and the cities. But we determined that our retirement future should be closer to our roots and families of origin.

We remembered the four relatively mild seasons in Southern Oregon: the budding pear and apple orchards of spring; rafting on the rivers and hiking in the evergreen forests during the summer; the brilliant autumn colors that invest the harvests and hills; and the comparatively moderate valley rains and mountain snows of winter. We longed to return to that environment and be enveloped in the welcoming arms of old friends and loving family members.

Our son was attending a West Coast medical school, and our daughter and her husband, a mathematician, were beginning their careers at a California university. So the pieces of our future retirement years were quickly falling into place. We were moving to Ashland, Oregon. But to our surprise, we were not destined to lead lives of sameness, lameness, and tameness. There were people in Ashland—diverse, interesting, exciting people—who would season our retirement experience with unforgettable and often amusing stimuli and adventures. So, rather than addressing retirement as an academic or theoretical subject (as I often did in earlier books), I have chosen an involved, subjective and spiritual approach—just as my wife and I are experiencing it.

While the familiar people, places, and events in our hometown form the context for the overall theme of our retirement transition, from time to time the narrative includes flashbacks to relevant childhood experiences. The human life course is a developmental and maturing process—physically, mentally, spiritually, and socially—as each of us moves seamlessly through the connected and related stages of childhood, youth, adulthood, and old age. At any stage, one's personality, perspective, and priorities may be perceived as the accumulating product of his or her past, unfolding life course. In other words, each of us has been profoundly socialized and shaped by a personal history. Thus, what the reader sees and hears today in the author's story is best understood when we realize that indeed, "*the child is the father of the man*" (William Wordsworth, 1770–1850).

# CHAPTER ONE

## The Professor and The Pines

I am a confirmed workaholic. All my life—from rural and small town childhood and youth, through college years of young manhood, and into a long teaching and research career as a university professor—I have heartily toiled at my assigned tasks. And I loved every minute with my hand on the plow, shoulder to the wheel, and eye on the prize. In short, the work ethic was my motivation, guide, and fulfillment.

Margaret and I never looked forward to that stage of life called retirement when golf, fishing, yoga classes at the senior center, and extended vacations would comprise our laid-back lifestyle. So while the slower, more recreational pace is undoubtedly beneficial to many retirees, we felt little desire to rest from the stimulating challenges of daily labor.

There was no compulsion from my university employer for me to retire at age sixty-five. In fact there are enough antiquated and tenured professors in their seventies and eighties doddering and puttering around the campuses to give life to the legend that "like old wine, cheese, and violins—professors seasoned by time can be in their most productive years."

Nevertheless, the emotional call of our West Coast family roots became more and more compelling. Our aged parents in California and Oregon deserved more of our presence. Our children completed medical school and graduate studies and had launched new careers in California and Washington State. And a new generation of grandchildren were arriving and tugging at our hearts. So the decision to sell our properties in the Midwest and initiate the retirement rituals was relatively easy.

Retirement from academe begins with the professor's letter to the university administration stating his reluctant intention to step down—embellished with superlative praises for many facets of his unforgettable experience at the university. The letter does not mention such mundane and chronic issues as the ubiquitous political jockeying and paltry financial rewards for merit. Rather, the retiree cites noble colleagues, the beautifully landscaped campus, and the latest exploits of our intrepid football team. [e.g., *"Go OSU Cowboys!"*].

In a week or two, a profuse and complimentary response arrives at the departing professor's office reluctantly accepting his resignation and expressing appropriate sorrow over the loss of an "irreplaceable" faculty member and his "epic contributions." For one brief, delirious moment the retiring professor fantasizes his honored name on a magnificent new building erected on campus. Perhaps his bronze statue heroically mounted on horseback would stand outside the entrance by a symbolic fountain of knowledge. The vision quickly fades in the light of reality.

The exit rituals are rather standardized and routine—including a departmental Faculty Farewell comprised of fruit punch, chocolate cake, and stale jokes. (For example: "Two aging professors are reading an announcement on a campus bulletin board when one remarks: Too bad about old Bynum—published and published—but perished just the same.") The highlight of the ceremony is the presentation of a distinguished achievement plaque bestowing the status of Honorary Professor Emeritus.

Clearing out one's office is a solo act. Personally removing my name from the office door was symbolic that my departure was voluntary and not forced—academic suicide is preferable over academic homicide. I gave away 150 books to doctoral students and shipped my lectures, publications, and the rest of my library to our future residence in Oregon. The large, plastic bone and the ominous sign over my desk that read "All that remains of the last student caught cheating on my exam" were bequeathed to a colleague. More seriously, I knew that I would miss my many marvelous students and our classroom journeys of academic discovery. As for me, like Columbus on his voyage to the New World, I was about to embark upon a new journey of retirement discoveries.

## The Reality of a New Habitat

Within two months, our long accustomed territory and habitat (Audrey 1966) changed from the halls and classrooms of Oklahoma State University, our small cottage near the campus, and a larger family home three hundred miles away in North Texas. Following my retirement and the liquidation of those properties, we discovered and purchased an older home on rural acreage near Ashland, Oregon.

The capstone on my academic career was two additional years as an Adjunct Professor of Sociology at Southern Oregon State University in Ashland. It was an appropriate and nostalgic farewell to my teaching career at the same institution where I began as a graduate student in 1968. At the same time, Margaret and I were falling in love with our one-hundred-year-old ranch house, surrounded by rolling lawns and a grove of giant, old-growth Ponderosa pine trees.

However, in spite of qualifying for the Oregon Historical Register and a faded sign in front by the flagpole identifying the place as The Pines, the buildings and grounds were in bad shape. It was definitely a fixer-upper. But the hint of a distinguished past and potential for restoration—plus a reasonable price—appealed to us. We excitedly closed the deal and moved in.

In some ways we were camping like pioneers in a rude and uncomfortable shelter. Before the house was livable, the leaking roof, dangerous electrical wiring, and dysfunctional plumbing required immediate repair. Shortly thereafter, I casually leaned on the ancient garage—originally designed for small, Model T Fords—and the old structure shuddered ominously. It took just four hours for a building contractor to knock it down and haul away the debris. In three more weeks, a large, red, barn–style, double garage and workshop—with a gambrel roof over the second-story carriage apartment—was erected on the site. Over the next four years, we restored the outbuildings, reseeded the lawn, repainted the fences, resurfaced the driveway, and rebuilt the place-name sign. And slowly The Pines emerged from many decades of wear and neglect and returned to the comfortable, old-fashioned appearance that it had back in the early twentieth-century.

## The Arborist

Then along came Woody—the arborist. I had invited him to evaluate the health and safety of the huge pine trees towering over the house. Woody was religiously dedicated to his specialty and took more seriously than I did the line from Joyce Kilmer's poem: "I think that I shall never see a poem as lovely as a tree" (Kilmer 1913). When I expressed concern for our lives if one of those big trees fell on the house, he replied without hesitation: "It would be a major tragedy to lose one of these trees."

Woody announced that the Ponderosa pines in our grove were rare survivors of an old growth forest that once covered the Rogue Valley before the nineteenth century logging industry harvested it to build cities and homes. A few small groves like ours had survived on private properties retained through successive family generations. In awe, Woody put our trees in historical perspective: "When George Washington was fighting the Revolutionary War in 1775, some of these trees were here!" He estimated their average trunk diameter at six feet and height up to 125 feet. The oldest Ponderosa pines in our grove are about three hundred years old.

The arborist made the rounds and reverently communed with each gigantic tree jn our grove, tentatively tried to identify the oldest paternal and maternal trees, and attributed individual characteristics to each one. As I watched Woody literally hugging the trees, I could almost hear him asking about the storms, droughts, and pine beetles they had endured and the vitality of their roots and sap.

## Change Is an Absolute

Our new home is only new to us. Its long history was again documented when we found stone mortars, pestles, and other ancient artifacts abandoned by Indians under the thick ivy at the base of one tree. We also dug up interesting old tools used by early white settlers in the area. Margaret and I are just the latest caretakers entrusted with this property. It seemed as old as dirt—inhabited by old trees, old buildings, and an old couple. And we have loved the on-going adventure of restoring and preserving The Pines! In it we found the retirement home of our dreams!

Personally, our retirement home forced me to transition from the tightly structured university schedule of fifty-minute class lecture/discussion periods, interminable committees meetings, and all-night research and writing marathons. I have been compelled to recall and revisit a much earlier and youthful time of my life when I worked on and with the land. And happily, I revised my expectation of the idealized, non-productive retirement to the more work-oriented, hands-on reality of my present retirement situation.

I discovered that advancing age and the restructured lifestyle associated with retirement required major modifications in my recreational plans. For example, with a sigh of relief, I excused myself from the joking agreement I had made with two younger colleagues to run with the bulls the following year in Pamplona, Spain. (They also changed their minds when they saw pictures of the large, horned brutes scheduled to pursue them on the Pamplona run!)

On the other hand, I truly regretted that my busy retirement schedule forced me to cancel a long- anticipated hike from Mexico to Canada on the rugged Pacific Crest Trail. In place of those potential adventures—and in harmony with my new lifestyle—I facetiously penciled in a visit to the annual Rooster Crowing Contest at Rogue River, Oregon, and momentarily considered membership in the Old-Timers' Whistling and Wood-Whittling Club.

## New Neighbors

Another early retirement discovery was that a host of other animal species also shared our new environment as home territory. And they are competing with us night and day for space and survival. This diversified zoo of wild animals came to my attention a day after we moved in when at about midnight, the motion light on the back patio was suddenly activated. Peeking through a window, I was astonished to see several raccoons and skunks partying around the picnic table. Although the lid on the garbage can was secured with a strap, the critters were merrily rolling it around the yard. During the following week, with the professional assistance of Pat the animal trap expert, we caught nothing except an angry fox that Pat released in the nearby hills.

A few days later, a visiting mountain lion—while casually hunting for breakfast in our neighborhood—aroused excited barking from a neighbor's dogs several acres away. The dogs had treed the snarling cougar next to a large barn where my neighbor—exercising the law of the jungle—executed him with rifle fire. I was saddened at the outcome because the cougar's ancestors were living here long before human intrusion.

With that historical perspective in mind, I tried to establish a cease fire and armistice with more formidable animal residents: They could make occasional raids on our apple and plum trees. (There were unsettling rumors of bears in the area.) For my part, I pledged to avoid confrontation with potentially aggressive animals and to refrain from carrying garbage out to the can after dark. In short, if they would stay out of my house, I would stay out of their way.

Harry Potts, our local game warden, advised me to carry a canister of bear spray to discourage a hungry bear that might cross my path. His suggested backup defense was to grab the nearest skunk as nature's best bear repellant. Considering the options, I decided that I preferred to wrestle a bear rather than a skunk. Regarding smaller predators, as a gesture of goodwill, I no longer stocked our small pond with goldfish, thus removing an irresistible fishing temptation for a neighboring raccoon family.

Our conflict of interests with deer and ground squirrels continued unabated—though their efforts to reproduce their numbers far exceeded my success in reducing their tribes. The deer have been so disrespectful and audacious that they feasted on dozens of expensive tulips, even with Margaret and me a few feet away. The ground squirrels—unlike their cuter tree squirrel cousins—foraged everywhere, even digging the delicious tulip bulbs out of the planters.

I tried many defensive responses—mostly unsuccessful. The deer eventually moved further up into the mountains as more people with family dogs moved into our area. Bambi and her fawns were cute, but one of those big bucks tended to shake his antlers in my direction. The adult deer could also easily jump a four foot fence. Hank Green at the Grange recommended a product containing cougar urine to repel unwanted deer and ground squirrels when they scented the presence of a natural enemy. I hesitated because of three haunting questions: (1) How was the cougar urine collected in the first place? (2) Would the lingering odor also repel us? And (3) While the cougar urine might repel deer, could it theoretically be attractive to unwanted real cougars? Those questions remained unanswered while I picked off a few ground squirrels with my .22-rifle.

The moles invade our property every spring, stay all summer, and hibernate somewhere during the winter. One or two enthusiastic moles searching for grubs, worms, and other insects can destroy a large lawn in two or three weeks. We tried a variety of unsuccessful strategies, including chewing gum and mothballs deposited in their burrows, carbon monoxide and other gases pumped into their underground tunnels, and water from garden hoses flooded into their holes. I even made a desperate but hopeful one-hundred-dollar investment at the local hardware store for sophisticated electronic devices to insert in mole holes. Theoretically, these battery-powered instruments are designed to emit high frequency noise that will irritate the moles and drive them off the premises.

With confidence in ultimate scientific victory, I carefully followed directions. But after two days, I was disappointed to see that the number of fresh mounds in my yard had tripled. Several moles even affectionately burrowed up next to the electronic devices! My test revealed that the electronic devices did indeed, have a profound effect on the marauding moles. They emitted a virtual call of the wild that was attracting moles from everywhere to a love-fest in my yard. My final solution was in direct hand-to-claw combat by placing mole traps in the burrows. The execution is bloody business, but the nine or ten moles I kill every summer with my traps—while not a total solution—is a partial control of their population and damage.

# I Wanted to "Know What the Wild Goose Knows!" (Gilkyson 1950)

We enjoy the colorful blue jays, robins, wrens, woodpeckers, and other wild birds that also seasonally share our ecosystem. The flights of honking Canadian Geese are especially fascinating to me. Many times I am spellbound when twenty or thirty of these splendid animals circle our home before landing near a large pond to rest and feed for a day or two before resuming their migration. The spell is always broken when they bombard my car with fresh fertilizer.

Unlike Henry David Thoreau, who moved to Walden Pond in search of transcendental enlightenment about his purpose in life, I spent a few hours at the Goose Pond to observe the intelligent and interesting social behavior of these magnificent birds. My visit was cut short by a swarm of ravenous mosquitoes that collected some of my blood in exchange for access to the geese.

The "following" behavior that characterizes geese and many other animals is demonstrated daily at the pond during the migration season. In the early twentieth century, the research of Konrad Lorenz produced graphic evidence supporting his hypothesis that the neural circuitry of newly-hatched goslings is not fully connected until they see and identify the nearest moving object as their parent (Lorenz 1981).

In order to test the hypothesis, Lorenz removed fertilized goose eggs from the parent's nest and placed them in an incubator. Shortly after the little goslings emerged from their shells, they observed the nearby figure of Konrad Lorenz. Instantly, Lorenz and his boots literally became Mother Goose. Subsequently, some amazing photographs show twelve young geese lined up and faithfully following Lorenz as he walked down a country lane. He named this biological/behavioral connection *imprinting*, which is critical to the survival of young animals of many species requiring a model and mentor.

I was also intrigued by the V formation flight pattern of migrating geese. Researchers have concluded that this standard formation is based on both instinct and experience in taking advantage of the collective lifting power in the wind current generated by their wedge-shaped formation.

Formerly, I thought that all the honking within a flight of geese came from the lead goose—the point bird in the formation. I assumed that he set the pace and direction and honked his signals: *Follow me! This is the way!*" However, authorities on goose behavior have since discovered that nearly all that honking comes from geese further back in the flight formation. A male chauvinist of my acquaintance added that all that honking must be "back-seat criticism from irate females complaining that the lead goose is flying recklessly, too fast, and in the wrong direction."

I previously read that geese are generally monogamous—that is, a mated pair usually stays together until one or the other dies. This finding was verified when I observed that a single goose seldom falls out alone from a flying formation. In nearly all cases, I witnessed dropouts occurring in pairs, with the companions resting and recuperating together on the ground before reconnecting with their original or another flight of geese.

I also witnessed a remarkable instance of prejudice and discrimination among a group of migrating geese temporarily resting at the pond. Before launching into the air for the next leg of their journey, a flight of Canadian geese will make several experimental, low-flying sorties to test and organize the flying formation before making the final decision to resume their journey.

For several days I had observed a large white goose mixing amiably with more common groups of brown Canadian geese on the banks of the pond. Clearly the white goose was of a different species—perhaps a snow goose that had become separated or lost from a flight of his own kinsmen. Somehow, the Canadian geese are able to signal or communicate with one another when they want to take a few circles in formation over our neighborhood. Apparently the white goose was not privy to the language or decisions of the Canadian geese, and he was surprised and agitated when the Canadian geese suddenly flapped their wings and took off together. As they circled the area, the white goose took a position on top of a large barn and indignantly honked at the flying Canadians every time they passed overhead. Obviously, while he was allowed to share their company on the ground, he was rejected as a flying companion. Birds of a feather do indeed, flock together.

# CHAPTER TWO

## Deviant Behavior

A shland, Oregon has a population of about 24,000 people that includes several thousand students at Southern Oregon State University and a large number of more affluent retirees from California and elsewhere. There are also many educational, medical, legal, merchant, and civil service professionals living in Ashland. Another small segment of the population is comprised of blue collar residents who generally commute to work in the nearby larger city of Medford.

Supplementing these city demographics is the annual influx of thousands of tourists—attracted by moderate temperatures, four distinct and beautiful seasons, classic plays, outdoor concerts, Rogue River excursions, the nearby Pacific Crest Trail, and winter skiing on snow-capped Mt. Ashland. Also, daily and casually sprinkled into the mix are numerous and transient street people—contemporary throwbacks to the hippie movement of the 1960s. Ashland's highly diversified population is guaranteed to produce an interesting and lively community.

The center of downtown Ashland is the picturesque and old-fashioned plaza—an open, triangle-shaped area around the pioneer statue and a fountain commemorating the eighteenth-century arrival of settlers to the Rogue Valley. Clustered around the plaza are small and diverse shops, cafes, and nineteenth-century–style street lamps, reflecting the small-town architecture and ambience of an earlier era. The adjacent world-class Shakespearean theater and beautiful, ninety-three acre Lithia Park are very popular.

The plaza is an appealing hub of interest and activity to the artsy tourist crowd. It is also the site of numerous public demonstrations ranging from the sober, black-robed Women for World Peace, to occasional speech-making by political candidates, to the seasonal gatherings of children celebrating Halloween or the arrival of Santa Claus, to several homeless, guitar-strumming vagrants bedding down for the night.

While the large majority of our town's inhabitants conform to dominant cultural expectations for clothing styles, behavior, and the basic values and traditions of the larger American society, there are still occasional and startling surprises. As a retired sociologist, one of my specialized areas of research and teaching focused on social problems and deviant behavior. Consequently, one could assume that I was prepared for any human anomaly or spectacle I might encounter. However, that illusion was soon replaced by the reality of Ashland, Oregon, as a dynamic sociological laboratory. To illustrate, three extremely colorful and unusual characters recently crossed my path.

## The Autumn Man

One October day, Margaret and I were taking our usual stroll along a remote trail in Lithia Park. Suddenly, ahead of us a strange apparition emerged from the trees and waited for us to pass. At first, I was startled. Thinking the creature might be a large animal, I looked around for a defensive stick or rock. But on closer inspection, we determined that it was a man—cheerfully greeting us as we passed on the trail. He was wearing a burlap coat and hat, bedecked head to toe with hundreds of colorful autumn leaves, interlaced into rough garlands of ivy, ferns, and other plant materials. It was our first encounter with the legendary and often-sighted Autumn Man who haunts the wooded environs of Lithia Park every fall. Autumn Man is a regular Ashland spectacle, apparently harmless, and readily posed for photographs from Margaret's camera.

## Lonesome John

Another well-known and recognizable Ashland resident is Lonesome John--a forty-year-old homeless panhandler. He customarily crouched in tattered rags at the entrance to a popular shopping mall where many passersby could observe his abject poverty. John's face, beard, and hands were encrusted with dirt. I witnessed passing motorists and pedestrians deeply moved by the scene as they thrust cash into John's trembling hands. Sympathetic good Samaritans often rushed warm meals to John as he took a break on his convenient rock at noontime.

John received more intense public attention when he lost control of a cooking fire next to the abandoned barn where he slept. A strong wind quickly pushed the growing fire through dry brush and burning embers jumped across the highway into the attractive Oak Knoll subdivision near the golf course. Before responding firemen could gain control of the situation, the conflagration had torched eleven homes. As evacuated residents surveyed the ruins of their destroyed homes, a report reached police that a disheveled figure was seen running away from the burning barn. They said: "It looked like Lonesome John!" (AP, August 25, 2010).

John was arrested under a bridge where he had taken refuge. He confessed his involvement in the fire and was incarcerated in the Jackson County jail. During the subsequent court proceedings, Lonesome John's responsibility for the fire was reduced because prosecutors did not prove he was aware of the dangers of his actions, a condition that needed to be met for a conviction of reckless endangerment. After a few months in jail he was released.

A few months later, John again raised public alarm when he was arrested and charged with endangering public safety by tossing three-foot orange traffic cones off an overpass onto Interstate Highway Five. This earned him several more months of confinement in jail (Guzik 2011). Before long, he was arrested again for allegedly throwing stones and menacing frightened girls walking to school. After another short sojourn in jail, Lonesome John again returned to the streets where he continues his panhandling activities (Specht 2011).

## Lady Godiva

The third example of extraordinary deviant behavior came peddling into view on an otherwise sunny and serene day in our hometown. Picture Jack and Margaret Bynum, conservative grandparents to whom breakfast at the International House of Pancakes and a visit to the Antique Mall could be a day to remember. We had been to the grocery store and were cautiously motoring down busy Siskiyou Boulevard through Ashland toward our rural home south of town.

Suddenly our calm reverie was abruptly shattered by the startling sounds of honking automobile horns, squealing brakes and tires, and shouts of pedestrians behind us. Looking back through my rearview mirror, I saw what appeared to be an unclothed woman approaching on a bicycle in the street. We were caught in slow-moving traffic, so the bicyclist quickly caught up and nonchalantly peddled alongside our car. Turning to my wife, I asked, "Do you see what I see?" Like most citizens, after our first embarrassed shock, Margaret and I were offended at the woman's scandalous contempt for generally accepted standards of public decency.

The most well-known precedent for this kind of behavior is found in the implausible eleventh-century legend of Lady Godiva, an Anglo-Saxon noblewoman married to the powerful Earl of Mercia. The story unfolds as Lady Godiva repeatedly implores her stubborn husband to lower the oppressive taxes imposed on his tenants. Finally the earl declares that he will lower the taxes when she rides naked on horseback through the streets of Coventry. He assumed that it was an impossible condition. Motivated by pity for the people, Lady Godiva purportedly asked all the residents of Coventry to stay in their houses and close all doors and shutters on a given day. When that was accomplished, Lady Godiva supposedly made her famous ride through Coventry, clothed in nothing but her resolve and long, flowing hair (Donoghue 2002).

Eleven centuries later, less modest and altruistic than the original Lady Godiva, Jill Melon moved from Southern California to Ashland, Oregon. A week before our encounter with Ms. Melon bicycling down Siskiyou Boulevard, she began her sojourn in our fair city with a visit to the police department where she inquired regarding nudity ordinances in Ashland. When officers informed her that public nudity was only restricted in parks, near schools, and in the downtown commercial district, witnesses reported that she turned a cartwheel in police headquarters. In just a few days, our new Lady Godiva took to the streets of Ashland to publically practice her nudism—to the mixed jeers and cheers of spectators. She contended that clothing was contrary to the natural, normal, and innocent lifestyle first demonstrated in the garden of Eden.

Some aroused citizens quickly declared that "Ashland is not the garden of Eden" and demanded stronger ordinances against public nudity from the city council—though a few liberal voices pointed to the woman's Constitutional freedom of expression. There followed a prolonged debate among the six-member city council. Our Ashland City Council has a record of dysfunctional bickering—at one time spending $37,000 in city funds for professional counseling on anger management and conflict resolution (Plain 2007). As they plodded along with the nudism issue, the Naked Lady threatened to seek support from the combative American Civil Liberties Union.

Finally, the city council reached a decision to ban full nudity in Ashland. Miss Melon countered with her application for an entry in the upcoming July 4 Independence Day Parade that draws thousands of spectators each year. The Ashland Chamber of Commerce learned of her parade plan from an online posting in which she promised to "lead a group of naked roller skaters"—with her blowing a conch shell to herald their arrival. This development was reported in detail by the news media and created quite a stir throughout the county. The upcoming parade was expected to achieve record attendance. (*The Daily Tidings* 2008).

City-wide attention was riveted on the Naked Lady as parade organizers searched for a way out of the dilemma of a naked group of skaters interspersed in the parade with marching school bands, flag-bearing veterans, clowns distributing candy to children, carloads of dignified city officials, and decorated floats containing Girl Scouts, Shakespearean actors, church groups, college athletes, and the newly crowned Miss Ashland.

Considering this potential spectacle, my friend Jasper offered a creative suggested: "If parade organizers are somehow obliged to admit the Naked Lady and her entourage of roller skaters into the parade, that entry should be placed at the very end—directly behind the three dozen horses." [The horses are traditionally grouped together at the end of many parades along with a clown "pooper scooper." This pragmatic sequence of entries places the accumulating contributions of fresh horse manure *behind* the marching bands]. One can only imagine the sensational parade finale as the naked roller skaters plow through all that fertilizer. "After all," Jasper argued, "The original Lady Godiva was certainly familiar with horses!"

Fortunately, such desperate measures were not needed. Parade organizers cited an established, time-honored policy governing parade entries that overruled the Naked Lady's petition: "All parade entries must comply with the standard of suitability for family viewing." After that setback, Ashland's Lady Godiva peddled (or skated) off into the sunset and has not been seen again in Southern Oregon. On the positive side, the startling, disgraceful, and ludicrous aspects of such local incidents drew residents and neighbors together in a common cause— and Margaret and I began to feel more comfortable as newly retired members of the community.

# CHAPTER THREE

## Flight 212: Seattle to Medford

Not all the unusual and unorthodox behavior in our hometown occurs among a few highly visible residents. After further observation and reflection, we concluded that unsettling conduct is more common than we first surmised. Even Margaret and I on occasion have contributed some instances of eccentric and even alarming performances on the public stage. For example, we suddenly and unintentionally became a center of public concern a few years ago at the Seattle International Airport. We had just concluded a pleasant one-week visit with our son Dan, his wife Sherri, and their children, and were scheduled to leave for home on flight 212: Seattle, Washington to Medford, Oregon.

Typically, there is always some potential stress at airports—among air controllers in the tower, baggage handlers and mechanics on the tarmac, and the milling throng of passengers in the terminal. A main source of stress is the security and boarding protocol. Large crowds of departing passengers are lined up for processing of tickets, checking luggage, acquiring boarding passes, and the removal of shoes and contents of pockets. Then the passengers are subjected to either a full-body X-ray or a personal pat down search for guns, knives, bombs, drugs, poisons, or other hidden contraband.

Margaret chose the X-ray—even after I reminded her of an unverified rumor that an electronic glitch might transmit her name and a revealing

X-ray picture throughout the airport on the ubiquitous flight schedule monitors. She bravely and stoically marched over to the X-ray booth. As for me, I was concerned that a lifetime of accumulating X-ray radiation would soon empower me to make long-distance calls without a telephone or open my electric garage door without using the remote control. So I was instructed by a young man to stand quietly with my feet planted on two painted footprints twenty inches apart on the floor. As the guy frisked my clothes and body for prohibited items, I could not help but wonder if he was just businesslike and thorough—or overly friendly and familiar. The politically-incorrect question crossed my mind and almost escaped my lips: "Are you gay?" However, he soon completed his task and waved us on toward our Alaska/Horizon airliner.

## Airport Syndrome

In just a minute or two, I suddenly felt strangely dizzy. I paused as I started to black out and called Margaret's name. The last thing I remember was a man's voice from behind me in the line: *"Will someone help this gentleman!"* I must have slumped down onto the terminal floor and soon found myself lying on my back, staring up into the faces of three members of the airport emergency response team. I managed to blurt out, "I am so sorry," to which one small boy pointed his finger and shrilled: "Look, Mommy! That grandpa fell down!"

The emergency response team quickly hooked me up to a portable oxygen tank and a blood pressure monitor and asked a series of questions to determine if I was injured, senile, psychotic, drunk—or just another clumsy old man who stumbled or fainted.

In order of importance and frequency, they inquired: "Do you have medical insurance? What is your name? Are you feeling any pain? Have you been drinking alcohol—or water? Did you eat breakfast this morning? Do you have medical insurance? What is your medical history? Heart disease? Low or high blood pressure? Strokes? Anxiety attacks? Can you count to ten? How many fingers am I holding up? Where are you going? Do you have medical insurance?"

The surrounding crowd watched and listened intently—reserving judgment on my guilt for anything other than my audacity for showing up at the airport. As was her custom, Margaret leapt into action by taking copious notes and calling our son on her cell phone: "Your father is lying on the terminal floor!"

By then, the emergency response team had discovered that I was breathing and my heart was beating. They were disturbed to find that my blood pressure had fallen to about 75 over 40. When I tried to rise to a more vertical position and stated: "I must catch a plane," they insisted that I remain on the floor. They officially notified me that I would need hospital clearance before I could be allowed on an aircraft. With that news, I was lifted onto a gurney and wheeled to a terminal side door where a waiting ambulance whisked Margaret and me to a Seattle hospital.

Two thousand dollars later—after a battery of tests, physical examination, extensive interview, and a meal in the hospital—I was diagnosed with the Airport Syndrome. That medical jargon usually stands for a temporary malfunction affecting elderly passengers. The cause is one or more of the following: suddenly lowered blood pressure, reduced blood sugar from skipping breakfast, dehydration from failing to drink water, and the stressful airport environment. An emergency room physician finally issued an official *"OK"* for me to fly—somewhat like the USDA symbol of approval routinely stamped on a slab of beef heading to the market. Everyone seemed relieved that I had medical insurance.

## The Suspicious Terrorists

Our expensive interlude at the hospital did not delay the flight from Seattle to Medford. The plane departed on time without us. Margaret and I stayed overnight at a nearby motel to await the Seattle to Medford flight scheduled the next day. At the appointed time we successfully repeated the detailed boarding protocol at the airport. Before I report what happened next, I must give a little background of Margaret's chronic medical problem.

My wife has been diagnosed with a weakened immunity disorder. This means that she is more vulnerable to colds, influenza, and other contagious diseases that may be free-floating among crowds of people. One sneezing, nose-blowing individual is a walking microbe factory who can potentially share his malady with scores of healthy people who transiently share his social space.

Most people with healthy immune systems will probably not catch the flu from that brief contact with a carrier. If they do contract the disease, it will mildly run its course in a few days. On the other hand, a person with a weakened immune system is not only more susceptible to the disease, but may go into pneumonia or some other life-threatening condition. For this reason, Margaret's doctors have advised her to avoid public places inhabited by crowds of people as much as possible during the influenza season. I also restrict my own exposure to crowds during flu season for fear that I might contract the disease and bring it home to Margaret.

As a compromise to avoid total isolation from society, Margaret's doctors also suggested that when mingling with crowds is unavoidable, she would be wise to wear a white medical mask over her mouth and nose.

As we maneuvered through the airport crowds, and to be doubly safe from invasive viruses, Margaret and I both donned our medical masks. We were relieved to join the line of passengers boarding Flight 212 that would finally carry us home! Suddenly, as we neared the airplane, an authoritative voice spoke over my shoulder: "What's with the masks?" Turning around, I was almost nose to nose with a cold-eyed, sharp-featured young man. He spoke through clenched teeth and had his right hand stuffed in a pocket of his buttoned-up trench coat, as if he was packing something other than bubble gum—maybe a stun gun or a high-caliber pistol. In short, he resembled Dick Tracy, the cartoon detective of my childhood. He was intimidating and unnerving, as he played the role very well. Obviously, he suspected us as terrorists or airplane hijackers trying to hide our identities behind the masks. I anticipated that he was about to command us to raise our hands above our heads and surrender. I feared another official pat down.

In retrospect, I can understand why he suspected us of being disguised terrorists. Although our pictures had not yet been posted on the WANTED BY POLICE bulletin board at the post office, we appeared very dangerous. In spite of her gray hair and spectacles, Margaret is a slender but tough holder of a black belt in knitting and baking cookies. As for me, obviously my arthritic limp is part of my cover. Working out on my riding mower in monthly lawn exercises has molded my body into steel. (My developing six-pack of abs are up to two). I have a neighborhood reputation as a cold killer of moles that are trying to destroy my yard.

Momentarily stunned, I stammered out my explanation to the officer: "My wife has a serious autoimmune problem and we are trying to protect her with a medical mask from possibly dangerous influenza viruses among the airport crowds. I am also wearing a medical mask because I don't want her to feel alone and conspicuous." Surprised, Dick Tracy stepped back and grudgingly muttered, "Have a nice flight, folks." Elated to be finally heading home, we boarded Flight 212, feeling that if we experienced any more excitement at the Seattle Airport I might faint again.

# CHAPTER FOUR

## Don't Eat the Oleanders!

Some of the lessons we first learned as children are soon forgotten. Others turn out to be guiding principles for the rest of our lives. I will never forget the points made by Miss Grace Twomley—our elementary school nurse in San Antonio, Texas. She was in her late thirties, never married, medically knowledgeable and efficient, and loved children. And we kids loved and respected Miss Twomley. Her plain little dispensary was just off the hall next to the principal's office. It contained a small table, large cabinet, a cot with blankets, three chairs, a telephone, a mysterious color chart on the wall of inside human anatomy, and Miss Twomley. In the cabinet was stored bottled water and an assortment of first-aid equipment—including bandages, splints, antiseptics, tweezers, thermometer, blood pressure monitor, several children's story books, and orange gum drops for the treatment of bumps, bruises, scraped knees, allergies, poison ivy, insect bites, splinters, blisters, nose bleeds, occasional head lice, and hurt feelings of the kids who came limping in for first aid. And Miss Twomley's patients always received kind words and a gentle touch.

### Health Emphasis Week

Health Emphasis Week was a regular part of the fall curriculum in which Miss Twomley met a hour each day with the entire student body to show old movies such as *The Prevention and Treatment of Dog Bites,*

*Injuries on the Playground*, and *The Dangers of Fireworks*. The highlight of the week was when our school nurse took to the stage to lecture on Children and Health. She identified healthy and unhealthy foods, explained why we must wash our hands, and demonstrated how to brush teeth with a mannequin. No child who was there will ever forget Miss Twomley's shrill introductory warning: *"Don't eat the oleanders!"*

That startling announcement was intended to get the attention of restless, distracted, elementary school students who seemed to be afflicted with a generalized Attention Deficit Disorder rather than an eagerness to learn the causes of diseases and hear the nutritional value of carrots and spinach. And Miss Twomley's alarming outcry about the danger of oleander bushes always brought the crowd to attention.

"What are 'oleanders?'" several students would anxiously ask. And Miss Twomley responded: "The green, flowering shrubs planted along the highway through town and on the median between the north and south lanes of traffic—and (ominously) in some of your yards at home." They are a hardy, decorative plant—but one leaf can contain enough toxin to kill a full-grown man (Fayobserver 2013). Hushed whispers rippled through the audience. We recoiled and looked at each other to ask: "Did you touch an oleander on the way to school this morning? Have you eaten the forbidden oleander? What was that green thing in the sandwich I had for lunch? Was it a familiar and friendly slice of pickle— or was it a poisonous oleander leaf?"

We curious boys always anticipated Miss Twomley's annual lecture on Sex Education. I imagine that the girls also looked forward to the topic—but I can't be sure because no one discussed the subject with the opposite sex. And besides, that supercharged topic required that boys and girls meet separately with Miss Twomley for our sex education. As I recall, other than some confusing language and vague sketches, all we carried away from Miss Twomley's remarks that day was her mysterious advice to respect what she called "the social and physical boundary line between males and females." We literally interpreted that to mean: "Don't get too close to those girls!" We boys—especially those of us without sisters in the family and already suspicious of girls—accepted Miss Twomley's word as gospel truth. Years later I learned that the girls had received similar advice from Miss Twomley—except applied to those strange creatures called boys. Those vague and basic instructions regarding boy/girl contacts prepared me for the rumored Ten-Foot Pole Regulation governing inter-gender relationships that I later heard in college (graphically described in a later chapter).

## The Enduring Lessons

The practical lessons from Miss Twomley became even more obvious over time. We would never forget her insightful, commonsense maxims about personal responsibility and environmental hazards at home, in the school bus, on the playground, almost anywhere that could endanger the health of unwary children. "Don't eat the oleanders!" cried Miss Twomley! "Think—and look before you leap!" cautioned our school nurse. "Take care of your body!" she warned us. "Avoid getting too close to those dangerous girls (or boys)" she advised. "Don't run on icy sidewalks or try to walk on water!" she warned. "Only the Lord can do that! You may fall and get banged up, and I will have to repair the damage. You might even drown, and I will phone the bad news to your parents!" A major part of Miss Twomley's nursing philosophy was to *prevent* potential damage or disaster to her young students before it happened.

Occasionally, someone would temporarily forget Miss Twomley's counsel—with predictable and unpleasant consequences. For example, my brother Bud learned from hard experience the folly of getting too close to a girl. At age thirteen, he was smitten by a cool classmate. Unfortunately, she was a girl who, by turning her dazzling dental braces on him with a beguiling smile, transported him to puppy love nirvana. Eunice also had a favorite horse named Old Dolly that she proudly rode around town after church on Sunday afternoons. She often passed our house and favored Bud with a few nice words and allowed him to pet the horse. Petting Eunice was off-limits, of course—but who would dare or desire such a hazardous experience after hearing Miss Twomley's lecture on the subject! It took just a few visits from Eunice and Dolly before Bud began disappearing on Sunday afternoons.

Our parents commissioned me to follow Bud and see where he was going. I discovered and reported to our parents that Bud was spending an hour or two every Sunday afternoon sweating and shoveled manure out of Old Dolly's barn stall and paddock. Poor Bud. He thought that he was in love and hardly noticed that he was developing blisters and permanent B.O. from constant exposure to all that horse manure. At first, during those manly labors, Eunice perched on a nearby fence, encouraging Bud with her presence!

The light of freedom from slavery began to dawn on Bud when Eunice didn't appear at many of his barnyard visits. She said she had to practice her piano lessons or go shopping with her mother. She would leave notes for him on the barn door with instructions about where to pile the horse manure; to carefully close the paddock; and put away the shovel before leaving. Finally, Eunice saddled up and went riding on Sunday afternoons. So even Dolly was not there to greet Bud, and he was alone with all that manure. Our dad then informed Bud: "That is why fishermen put a worm or lure on the hook before inviting the fish to dinner." So Bud left a note on the barn for Eunice: "I'm tired of shoveling horse manure for you." Before long, Eunice slithered up to Bud at school, batted her eyes, smiled demurely, and said: "How are you, Bud? I have missed you at the barn." And I was so proud of my brother when he answered, "That smells a lot like horse manure to me" and bravely moved back across Miss Twomley's boundary line.

## Miss Twomley and Water Hazards

Although many years have passed, much of Miss Twomley's sage advice has continued to reside in the vivid memories of her many students—now grown into adulthood and even old age. For instance, one of her most enduring warnings came rushing into my mind during a recent visit to a large department store. I was confidently striding through the shoe department when I suddenly tumbled head over heels before my seventy-five-year-old bones landed in a heap on the hard floor. There were no caution signs alerting customers of slippery vinyl flooring, nor did I notice the janitor walking just ahead of me with a mop and bucket of soapy water.

As surrounding customers gasped in surprise and concern, I momentarily took inventory of various body parts before starting to get up. Contrary to customers' common failure to find a clerk for a price check or directions to the rest room, I became the instant focus of store personnel. The first thing I heard was a very loud announcement over the store public address system: "Code Thirty! Code Thirty! A senior gentleman has fallen in the shoe department!" Margaret—who was independently shopping in the sewing and fabric department—instinctively thought: *That sounds like Jack*, and headed for the shoe department.

Strangely, the voice of Miss Twomley echoed from the long ago memory of a school boy: *I told you, Jack Bynum! Don't run on the ice! And don't try to walk on water! Only the Lord can do that! You may fall and break your leg!* About then the store manager and a squad of well-coordinated clerks converged on my prostrate form. "Don't get up, Sir! Please stay where you are" they commanded. At first I surmised: *How thoughtful. They want to make sure I am not injured and in need of medical help.* Then I realized that I was about to witness a microcosm of the work ethic and the spirit of capitalism (Weber 1958) in which the working class rally to preserve and protect the profits of Big Business. Metaphorically, I saw the worker bees reinforce the queen bee and surround the hoard of honey against a potential threat to the hive.

Simultaneously, clerks began deploying orange safety cones all around my body. They were conspicuously marked CAUTION! WET FLOOR! Then the manager pulled out a camera and took pictures of me from all angles. [I forgot to smile for the pictures.] Clearly, they had established and documented evidence that the store was blameless, and I had blundered into a well-marked and potentially hazardous area. In any possible or resulting litigation, the corporate headquarters could reasonably claim that the store was the victim of an exploitive, conniving customer. Though highly embarrassed, only my dignity was wounded. I scrambled to my feet and quickly exited the store.

## A Fitting Eulogy

There is a happy ending to this story. A surviving group of elderly alumni of our old elementary school are hoping to install a small stone memorial on the campus dedicated to the memory of a beloved childhood friend. The appropriate inscription would simply state: "In Honor of Miss Grace Twomley, School Nurse: 1934–1956, *'Don't eat the oleanders!'*"

# CHAPTER FIVE

## The Family Necktie

Now that I am older and can take the long view of my life, I want to clarify certain points made in anecdotal reports to younger generations of the family regarding my childhood tribulations during the difficult economic depression of 1930–1940. My motive was to motivate the children to more zeal in their school work and home chores by comparing their hardships with mine at their age. In looking back, it is possible that those traumatic childhood experiences may continue to affect my life today.

Without doubt, those were difficult times, but my story to the children of "walking long distances through heavy snow drifts—uphill in both directions to and from elementary school" may require a little clarification. Some have questioned why the daily distance traveled has grown from three miles to six miles through repeated narrations over the years. For a mathematical explanation, perhaps I subconsciously changed from the American system of calculating distance in miles to the French metric system of computing distance in kilometers. Thus, in my later recollections of distance to school, I may have been using the metric system in which a kilometer is equivalent to about two-thirds of a mile. My second possible answer is simpler and easier to understand: As I have aged and my memory and physical stamina have declined, the distance between home and school seems longer now.

Other critics have challenged my reference to "heavy drifts of snow" encountered on my hikes to school as difficult to accept. The reason, they say, is because my early childhood was spent in San Antonio, a city in Southern Texas—a city with mild winters and very little snow. I can easily counter that contention with data from the Farmer's Almanac that documents a one-half-inch snowfall in San Antonio in 1933, when I was three years old. I assume that these logical counterarguments have reinforced the credibility of my memories relayed to children and grandchildren.

## The Family Necktie and Shoes

Without qualification, I am sticking to my account of family poverty involving the necessary sharing of clothing. For example, we had just one family necktie. It was brown with a white flash of lightning decorating the front. For years, Dad wore it to church, funerals, weddings, and other formal occasions. Over time, our family necktie accumulated a lot of mileage and soup stains. Nevertheless, we have photographic evidence of each of us boys, in turn, proudly wearing that family heirloom as we participated in our respective eighth-grade and high school graduations.

Undocumented, but still enshrined in family history, is how we stoically shared our shoes during the Great Depression. Leather shoes were expensive purchases for families of modest income, so we young boys often went barefooted Dogpatch-style (Capp 1934) during the summer months. During the nine-month elementary school year, we wore inexpensive tennis shoes (now known as sneakers). Dad had his heavy work boots and a pair of aged, black leather dress shoes that he wore on special occasions. In my early teens, I would borrow Dad's dress shoes for those social events that required formal attire. My younger brother Bud would do the same. There was no problem unless both of us attended the same event. In that case, Dad suggested that we could each wear one of his leather dress shoes, matched with one of our own tennis shoes. This was called Family Shoe Emergency: Plan B.

I suspect that readers may find this family plan for sharing shoes hard to believe, but those were hard times, and we learned to adapt. It was embarrassing at first, but depravation can develop character.

Our emergency Shoe-Sharing Plan was the origin of the well-known American adage: "Always put your best foot forward."

Our father was a resourceful man and also came up with a flexible Plan C backup" in case all three of us needed to attend events such as family reunions or formal weddings at the same time. Dad had primary use of his dress shoes while we boys could use his work boots, our own tennis shoes, go barefooted, or substitute some of Mom's high-heeled shoes. Fortunately, such critical situations happened only two or three times. Everyone vividly remembers how Bud was caught in a Plan C situation and had to wear Mom's high heels to his high school senior prom. But we learned that something good always comes from adversity. The school paper later reported that my brother was a sensation on the dance floor. Nevertheless, we were so happy when the Great Depression finally ended and we attained steady employment, a reliable income, and the beginnings of a middle-class lifestyle.

~

## An Afterthought

Several authorities on the effects of childhood trauma have suggested that some Depression-era children may have been emotionally scarred by the poverty they experienced in the 1930s. They have sought to trace the contemporary fear of economic collapse manifested by some older people to the earlier poverty they experienced during the Great Depression. It may be true! To this day, when I am struggling to balance our family budget, I occasionally catch a brief vision of myself walking down a lonely railroad track, destitute and hungry, barefooted, and wearing the family necktie!

# CHAPTER SIX

## Dinner Is Served—But
## Hold the Rhubarb!

Ten years ago—but the memory is so traumatic that it still seems like yesterday!—a colleague at Southern Oregon State University and his wife invited Margaret and me to be their guests at a newly- opened Japanese restaurant. At that time we knew very little about Japanese cuisine. So with some mild trepidation, we accepted the invitation, thinking we could eat a few vegetables and fruits and avoid any mysterious or scary items such as squid or octopus.

On the appointed evening, our hosts picked us up with excited promises of gourmet delights awaiting us at the Authentic Far-East Grill. Upon arrival, we were ceremonially ushered to our seats by an oriental maiden in a flowered kimono at a huge four-foot by eight-foot sizzling hot grill. Since we lacked experience and expertise in the cuisine or language of Japan, we blindly bluffed our way through the menu before placed our order for a dinner that vaguely appeared long on bamboo shoots. Our hosts smiled as they anticipated the dining pleasure ahead for us.

At the sound of a brass gong, two colorful Samurai-type cooks carrying large knives took positions on either end of the grill. There, with appropriate grunts, growls, and grins, they began chopping and flipping vegetables, whole fish, shrimp, tofu, and bamboo back and forth and in all directions. Margaret and I were spellbound until a sizzling, half-cooked shrimp landed in my ear—reminding me of my long-standing dining principle that nothing with eyes goes on my plate that may be watching me.

Finally, with a flourish, our steaming dinners were presented. After muttering a fatalistic banzai—(suicidal battle cry of charging Japanese soldiers during World War II)—Margaret and I gingerly picked through the meal. We concentrated on our new found fondness for parsley, tofu, and bamboo shoots. I am happy to report that we survived the dinner at the Japanese grill—but our hosts never again invited us to dine with them.

## The History and Culture of Food

In retrospect, that unforgettable dining adventure set me to thinking about our preoccupation with food. Our natural interest in satisfying the nutritional needs of our physical bodies dates back to when each of us entered this world. We were born hungry—with an insatiable appetite that would structure each day of our lives around breakfast, lunch, and dinner. But the important historic and cultural contexts and meanings of our food consumption warrant closer examination.

The history of humanity charts the utilitarian role of food as a vehicle enhancing significant events, or as a corollary to celebrations and rituals. For examples—how many birthday and wedding cakes, Easter eggs, and Valentine's candies have you consumed during your life? And how many turkeys and ducks have been invited to your Thanksgiving dinners?

On the international stage, food has played a major part in the rise and fall of kingdoms and empires—ranging from the historic sieges and starvation of fortified cities, to the wholesale slaughter of Buffalo herds by American pioneers on the Great Plains—followed by famine among aborigine Indian tribes, to the crop failures in parts of contemporary Africa. In 1790, Napoleon Bonaparte succinctly credited his military success to well-fed troops when he declared: "An army marches on its' stomach."

Beginning about 200 BC, the European market for spices from India led to exploration and travel over the famous Spice Trails across Asia Minor. In more recent centuries, the insatiable quest for tea from China and coffee from South America led to more world-wide commerce. Almost lost in the adventures of the mutinous crew of *HMS Bounty* is the original purpose of the voyage to study "bread fruit"—a staple on some Pacific islands—as a possible source of inexpensive food for British subjects in other parts of the world.

The importance of food to human survival can lead to extraordinary rationalization. For instance, in 1909, when Admiral Robert Peary and his small group of Arctic explorers were separated by storms and great distance from their supply resource, there was little hesitation about sacrificing some of their sled dogs. Peary later wrote: "Many times I sat down to a dinner of dog." And two continents away, the blood-curdling battle cry of one hungry, cannibalistic, African tribe was *"Food!"*—which undoubtedly energized both the attackers and the defenders (for different reasons) in the subsequent melee.

The sacred writings of every major religion are full of references to food—like huge menus spread across the millenniums of time. There are serious mandates prescribing or proscribing dietary practices—including our relationships with "sacred" cows, "unclean" pigs, "fatted" calves, and fish on Friday. The unfolding Old Testament story begins with the "forbidden fruit," moves on to "famine in Egypt," followed by the "land of milk and honey." The New Testament includes the miraculous "loaves and fishes," the Lord's Prayer request: "Give us this day; our daily bread," the sacred Last Supper, and countless other food references.

Today, food is clearly an important and intrinsic element in all the cultures of the world. Most national societies are identified and characterized by popular, traditional foods. For examples, Italians are famous for their pasta and pizza dishes; Mexican tortillas and chili are now popular everywhere; Chinese immigrants brought chow mien and chop suey to the Western world; and Russian caviar (sturgeon fish eggs) has become a popular and expensive food in many countries.

At the individual and personal level—young children are generally socialized regarding the importance of food. We were often admonished to "clean up our plates because the children in China are starving!"—to which one unusually precocious kid purportedly responded: "They can have this!" Later we were taught by precept and example to blindly swallow anything set before us by dinner hosts—even if it could gag a maggot—while gratefully exclaiming: "Hmmm! Yummy! Thank you!" The ultimate symbolic association between the human life course and food is acted out in many prisons when condemned men are asked to designate their last meal before going to the execution chamber.

## Rhubarb

My compliant and conforming attitude regarding food went with me to college in Northern California. During my junior year, I traveled up to Oregon to get acquainted with my future wife's family. During that initial visit in the Clary home, Margaret's mother engaged me in an exploratory dialogue that would have serious, long-range repercussions. Mrs. Clary was an excellent cook, and she wanted to find out my favorite and less desirable foods. It was obvious that she wanted to serve pleasing fare to her prospective son-in-law. She asked me to identify several of my favorite foods, to which I readily responded.

Then she inquired about those foods that least appealed to me. Again I supplied a short list of four or five foods that, to me, were too repulsive for human consumption. On the latter list of disliked foods, I gave prominence to rhubarb—a vegetable stalk apparently popular with everyone except me. Mrs. Clary then rushed off to the market as I silently rejoiced over the future prospects of many appetizing meals from the Clary kitchen.

However, that conversation was the seedbed for a dining disaster that would be visited upon me for many years. Somehow, my future mother-in-law got one item on the wrong list. Specifically, rhubarb wandered off the list of Jack's Disliked Foods and reached the top of the list of Jack's Favorite Foods. From that day forward, rhubarb was featured countless times on the Clary menu—in my honor! During subsequent years, when the news reached Ashland that Jack and Margaret were coming for a visit, Margaret's mother put in a large stock of rhubarb.

I could not complain for fear of hurting the feelings of my mother-in-law, who made such an effort to supply my culinary delights. In my wildest nightmare, I never imagined that rhubarb could be served in so many ways. It can be cooked or stewed, and baked in cakes, pies, and even cookies. I was often served rhubarb in all of these forms, much to Margaret's amusement. For someone who hates rhubarb, I have probably enthusiastically eaten more of it than anyone in the world. On two occasions, I desperately fed rhubarb cookies under the table to Mrs. Clary's dog. Later, when the dog died, I secretly wondered if her demise was from natural causes, murder (rhubarb poisoning), or suicide.

## Camel Cheese

I first began to modify my automatic thankful praise for whatever food was set before me on a 1966 trip to the Middle East. On one memorable occasion, our party of American tourists mounted camels for a caravan ride around the great Pyramids of Egypt. It was a relief to dismount from the temperamental, complaining brutes when we arrived at our desert encampment for the night. We settled down in a large ornate tent for a feast prepared by our Egyptian guides.

One of the new and surprising food items presented by our hosts was camel cheese, based on milk derived from our recent transportation, parked and lounging just outside the tent. I realized that our Egyptian hosts were expecting us to gratefully wolf down this unusual food (to Western palates). In an effort to be polite in a foreign culture—and for fear of insulting them and risking an international incident—I did manfully try. But the sight, smell, and taste of the camel cheese was just too close to its' camel source. After one or two half-hearted attempts, I experienced a temporary and partial paralysis when my arm was unable to convey the morsel of camel cheese to my mouth. In addition, I was suddenly afflicted with a form of psychological lock-jaw when my mouth would not open to receive the cheese.

The next day we visited the famous Cairo museum that houses an amazing collection of ancient Egyptian mummies. As our tour guide waxed eloquent over the life and death of a young pharaoh named Tutankhamen, I received an illuminating medical insight. The guide mentioned that a great mystery surrounds the death of King Tut. According to artifacts left with the body in the tomb, the teenage monarch spent much of his time dashing around the capital city on his golden chariot and eating, drinking, and partying until death suddenly intervened. Students of Egyptology have speculated that Tut may have suffered a fatal scorpion or serpent bite, a gastric disorder, or been poisoned by jealous competitors in a palace conspiracy.

No one really knows why King Tut died at such an early age. But the words *gastric disorder* and *poisoned* stuck in my mind. There may have been an abundant source of food poison shuffling right outside the palace kitchen. A herd of dusty, fly-infested camels were giving their all to produce camel cheese. Having tasted it myself, I can believe that it might have killed King Tut! I have considered sharing this new explanation of Tutankhamen's demise with mystified Egyptian scholars, but I am still concerned about causing an unsavory international incident.

## Broccoli

As I have entered my senior years, I have become more emboldened and decisive in expressing my food preferences. After all—why should I be bullied by society's food police during my retirement? There are heroes to emulate in this taste bud rebellion. George Herbert Bush ended his public career as a strong and forthright decision-maker. Leaving his World War II service as a fighter pilot and four years as president of the United States out of the equation, I have symbolically knighted "Sir George" for his defiant announcement to governmental officials and members of the press corps assembled in the White House Rose Garden:

> "All my life I have suffered the indignity of having
> to eat broccoli because it was 'healthy' or 'politically
> correct.' I am finally old enough to publically liberate
> myself from that unattractive and distasteful food."

While the nation was temporarily shocked at the president's audacity—especially the producers of broccoli—millions of sympathetic citizens recalled their own struggles to go against public pressure and cultural traditions by openly asserting their personal food preferences. There was no civil unrest, downward plunge of the stock market, or rioting in the streets in response to the President's announcement. But the enduring lesson remains for all of us: "Speak up before you throw up!" I too am now older and wiser. And I am standing in my own humble rose garden to publically join the former president of the United States in a call for Freedom of Taste!

# CHAPTER SEVEN

## New Problems, New People, and a New Perspective

When I left my teaching career and moved away from the university "halls of Ivy," my functional association with a social network of administrators, secretaries, clerks, teachers, and students was irrevocably terminated. And I was lonely for my former colleagues, students, and the classroom teaching role. There would be no more occasions for me when faculty members—looking dignified and robed in their academic regalia and square hats—marched in the graduation processional. [It would take a while before I realized that there was too much pomp for those circumstances].

My loneliness for my former life began to fade soon after we moved into our retirement home and became socially involved in our neighborhood, church, and community. An important key to meeting and interacting with new people was the ongoing and challenging repair and maintenance issues involving in making The Pines our home.

As the weeks passed, I developed easy rapport and first-name relationships with a large group of tradesmen and blue-collar workers— the personification of the theoretical *division of labor* that sociologists like to analyze (Durkheim 1997). There was Earl the electrician, Pete the plumber, Gus the handyman, George the garbage truck driver, Rodney the roofer, Fred the furnace serviceman, Walt the irrigation water master,

Charlie the carpenter, Sparky the tractor repairman, and so on. During their visits to The Pines, we exchanged pleasantries about our wives and children, homes and worries, and news and views regarding political and economic conditions.

I soon shed the burden of my former role as professor or doctor as my new working class colleagues simply called me by my familiar first name of Jack. Generally, I found these men to be humorous, intelligent, informed, articulate, honest, and refreshingly straightforward. In many cases, they became significant new friends and associates. Without any effort or adjustment, I happily returned to the practical, working class roots and role of my younger years. More and more I found myself visiting their shops and hanging out at Home Depot, the Grange, and Ace Hardware. My new lifestyle proved interesting, exciting, and far from boring.

## New Problems

When we first moved into The Pines, I occasionally hired relatively inexpensive workers from a labor contractor to help with the yard work. I soon discovered the variability of quality among day laborers. Some were diligent, responsible, and earned their wages. But others could be ranked on a scale of slow, slower, and comatose—requiring constant supervision. My use of that source of inexperienced and/or unreliable labor came to the end after I allowed a worker who claimed proficiency in operating farm equipment to use my new and beloved John Deere lawn tractor. Just to be safe, I gave him a few instructions such as: "Never drive over a water hose with the tractor's mowing blade engaged."

I had no sooner turned my back when I heard the terrible sound of grinding metal and broken parts flying off the tractor. Turning around, I beheld a disaster. The worker had run over a hose conveying water under strong pressure to several lawn sprinklers. About twenty-five feet of severed hose and a sprinkler head were wrapped around the smoking underside of the tractor. The twenty-five feet of hose still attached to the water valve and under pressure was whipping around like an angry python and spraying water everywhere. I turned off the water valve and removed the stunned driver off the stalled tractor. He was sent back to the labor agency, and the tractor was sent to John Deere for repairs. The lesson I learned from the experience was that we usually get what we pay for." A little more money hired my regular, long-time, efficient yard-man and friend.

I also made my own share of embarrassing mistakes. When I was more agile, I often climbed up on the roof of the house to remove accumulating leaves and pine needles with my blower. It was a quick and simple task, except the day when a gust of wind blew over the ladder leaving me trapped on the roof. It so happened that Margaret had gone shopping with one of her lady friends. Thus, there was no one else at home to hear my calls for help. So I sat on the roof—slowly baking in the summer sunshine for two hours before I tried shouting to occasional joggers passing on the road in front of our property. Most of them did not hear me. A few who did hear my call for assistance must have thought I was insane or a criminal and quickened their pace. Finally one curious man came and put up the ladder so I could come down from the roof. Thereafter, I always try to have my cell phone in my pocket. When I reached my eightieth birthday—and after a brother-in-law fell off his roof and broke several bones—Margaret grounded me from any more roof or tree-climbing adventures.

## Collective Teamwork

The sharing of certain memorable experiences at The Pines bonded a kind of camaraderie with some workmen. For example, one day two hired men were pruning trees and clearing brush on the property. One of them, Miguel, and I will never forget what happened when he trimmed and thinned the thick ivy that had accumulated around the lower trunks of some of the big trees. Margaret was in our living room when she heard Miguel shrieking from the front yard. I rushed from my study to see the man striking himself in a frenzied race around the house. Margaret yelled, "Jack, something has happened to Miguel! Help him!"

My initial thought was that the man was suffering a seizure. Rushing into the yard, I learned that Miguel had accidentally dislodged a large hornet's nest under the ivy, and the angry insects had swarmed to the attack. As I retreated from the scene of battle, I got stung several times on my hands and backside. Upon reaching the safety of the house, I shouted to Miguel, who was still running around the yard, *"Get into the workshop or your car!"* After the hornets finally broke off their attack, we were able to get the man into the house for some first aid.

Then I noticed that even though most of the hornets that had attacked poor Miguel had returned to their nest, one or two squadrons continued reconnaissance patrols in the yard and around the house. Unlike bees— who damage their stinger and die from their first attack— hornets can figuratively reload for subsequent assaults. The other workman, from his relative safety in the barn, ascertained the situation and shouted a request: "If someone can distract the hornets for a few minutes, I can make a run for the house."

I briefly considered the strategy of distracting the hornets. We had just witnessed the determined commitment of the hornets when in attack mode. And Miguel had proved beyond question that the hornets could not be outrun or deterred by screaming at them. I also recalled watching the behavior of lions at a zoo when a meal of fresh meat was thrown into their cage. Their dangerous predatory instinct and response was awesome.

With this evidence in mind, I shouted back to the man hunkered down in the barn, "I suggest that you stay where you are—unless you choose to remove your shirt and come out. I am confident that would distract the hornets for a while from the rest of us." He decided to stay in the barn until all the hornets returned to their nest.

Meanwhile, Margaret and I kept a low profile indoors until Stan the pest control expert arrived. Wearing his protective helmet, face mask, gloves, and heavy canvas suit, he looked like an alien visitor from Mars. However, with smoke wand and poison in hand, Stan expertly eliminated the nest of hornets. My workers are now more careful when poking around in unfamiliar places and spaces.

---

On another occasion, without any overt symptoms or warning, one of our old ponderosa pine trees suddenly died. As its green needles turned brown and the bark took on a gray hue, the big tree became a genuine hazard and required professional removal. We did not dare report our decision to Woody the arborist because his sensitive nature would have been traumatized by the demise of the tree. But the removal of the huge dead tree near our home gave us the opportunity to witness the fantastic skill of professional loggers. Their contracted assignment was to top and drop the massive tree in a narrow, designated area without damaging the house, outbuildings, rail fence, and especially Margaret and me.

Mel, Ross, and Clyde arrived with their ropes, pulleys, chain saws, climbing shoes, and an abundance of bravado. They began by rigging a leather harness near the top of the targeted tree. As I watched them, my first impression was that they were either drunk or crazy, or both. With my camcorder running, I filmed one Tarzan–type logger skillfully work his way up the lofty pine, cutting off limbs with his chain saw as he ascended. Finally—after showing off with acrobatic swinging upside down in his harness and much shouting and joking with his companions on the ground—he deftly cut off the top twenty feet of the pine. He then descended to join his fellow loggers in studying the logistics involved in dropping the tree within the prescribed perimeters.

The loggers then became more serious, and it was apparent that they perceived the felling of a great tree as almost an art form. Margaret and I were banished to the protection of the house. After making methodical, carefully calculated notches with an axe, incremental cuts with a very large chain saw, the systematic insertion of wedges of different sizes, and frequent checking of wind direction and angle—the old pine tree leaned over and returned to the earth from which it had first emerged three hundred years ago. It fell with a mighty crash.

Some philosopher once conjectured: "If a tree falls in the forest and no one is present to hear it, does it still make a noise?" Sound recording instruments left in remote forests and mountains, and on islands without human habitation, revealed that storms still raged, thunder still rumbled, and trees still fell with an awesome noise. After witnessing the final capitulation to death by the ancient and noble tree in my yard, I believe there would always be a crashing farewell—even in a forest without the presence of mankind. It would be heard by the Creator of the world who loves all the products of His divine handiwork—including men and trees.

As we surveyed the fallen giant in the yard, I broke out some cans of cold root beer to celebrate with the logging crew. (It was the closest I could come to their favorite kind of brew.) They had successfully dropped the tree within six inches of my designated spot on the ground. The celebration was a kind of guy-thing!

Next on the agenda was the removal of the fallen tree from my property. I brought in Bill with his remarkable portable mill. In three days of hard work he transformed that big old pine into enough lumber (studs, joists, and rafters) to frame four new houses. Bill hauled away half of the new lumber as his fee. After a period of drying, I sold most of my half of the lumber and gave away the last remaining pieces to friends.

There were several instances at The Pines when major problems were of such magnitude and complexity that the expensive coordination of workmen with different specialties was necessary for resolution. (I soon learned that an open mind and open checkbook can solve most problems of this kind.) For example, I will never forget the emergency telephone call I received from the City of Ashland Water Department. Although we live in Jackson County outside the Ashland city boundary, we are still conveniently serviced with city water for household use. This telephone message is dreaded by every homeowner:

"Our meter reader has found a serious water leak on your property. Thousands of gallons of water have already escaped the system. Major water damage to your home is very possible. We have determined that this water leak in not on the city service line that delivers water to the meter on the front edge of your property. Water is then redistributed by your pipe system throughout your property. The leak is somewhere in your system and falls within your responsibility. Please report to us right away what steps you are taking to control this serious water leakage."

I ran out to the water meter to verify what I had just heard. And sure enough, my heart sank when I saw the usage indicator on the water gauge (that normally moves at a very slow rate) racing out of control. I turned off the main water valve and made several emergency telephone calls for help. Within forty-five minutes, reinforcements began to arrive.

Pete the plumber got there first and immediately crawled under the house checking pipes for signs of leakage. My insurance agent Sherman lives nearby and took a prayerful vigil on the porch while contemplating what this event might cost his company. An environmental safety officer from the county showed up because water leaks of such magnitude could result in a dangerous sink hole. That possibility really alarmed me. We heaved a sigh of relief when the plumber reported that he found nothing abnormal under the house and that a resident snake, skunk, and family of spiders seemed unconcerned. I next called a professional water leak detection company that dispatched Tim and Joe to our property. The work of these expert water finders is a little like *water witching*—but with the assistance of scientific instruments to track down the water leak in an uncharted maze of old pipes around our one-hundred-year-old residential property.

Tim and Joe deployed their antenna and electronic acoustic leak detectors wherever they thought underground water pipes might exist. Water rushing from a broken underground pipe is characterized by an unusual hissing or whooshing sound. In order to magnify the sound and identify the exact underground spot to the men listening above, sensitive amplifiers were systematically moved from place to place on the ground surface. It was a slow, painstaking procedure—with my handyman and two plumbers standing by to quickly dig up and replace the broken pipe when discovered. And it was getting expensive. As taxi passengers are always aware: "The time meter is running!"

Finally, and suddenly—the electronic water detectors' signaled and identified the location of the leaking underground pipe. The plumber and his assistant began digging and soon uncovered their objective about eighteen inches underground. Water was pouring from an old disintegrating pipe. The water valve at the meter was again turned off while the plumber replaced and sealed the broken pipe. One of the men was stationed at the meter when the water was turned on again. When he observed that the needle on the water usage gauge had stopped spinning wildly, he let out a shout of victory and raised his arms overhead like a football referee signaling a touchdown! We all joined in the celebration.

In a few days the shocking bill arrived from the city water department. The huge amount of water lost through that broken pipe cost over $1,100. When I complained to the water department, a clerk pointed out that the water event on my property was an act of God, and the charges were legitimate. I was upset at that disclaimer and suggested that they should therefore, "send the bill to God." Further negotiation reached a more equitable resolution: The water company would split the water charge with me—fifty/fifty. I also received a major discount from the water leak detectors, and my handyman donated his services. My insurance company also helped cover the plumbing expenses. So—as Shakespeare wrote: "All's well that ends well!" (Shakespeare 1994).

~

## A New Perspective

Margaret and I are thoroughly enjoying our retirement years. This exciting stage of our life course has been filled with new challenges, new people, and new fulfillment. We have continued to grow mentally, socially, and spiritually. We face the future with cheerful optimism and faith. Among our many happy discoveries is the growing awareness that God is literally and practically involved in our personal welfare. There is abundant evidence that a Higher Power is actively smoothing out the rough spots along the way and giving us little and large blessings every day.

For example, with advancing age, both of us have developed chronic arthritis. Our experience seems to confirm the old adage that sudden changes in barometric pressure can enable some folk with bad knees to predict impending changes in weather. It does seem that some days we experience a bit more pain and stiffness in our legs when a storm is approaching.

Our inability to walk as well as we did a year or so ago prompted Margaret and me to look for empty parking spaces close to the stores where we shop. There are usually a few parking spaces designated for people with medical problems, but these are usually already filled when we arrive. One day as we were parking some distance away from the store, I facetiously remarked to Margaret: "We need an angel to intervene in such situations and help us find a parking place closer to the stores." It was not a prayer requesting any help. It was just an informal observation. We dismissed that stray thought and went on about our shopping. But apparently the Lord took the matter seriously! I am not making this up.

The next day when we entered a parking lot and approached the main store entrance, a strange man stepped in front of our car and repeatedly motioned us into an empty parking spot that was very close to the store. We didn't think any more about that fortunate circumstance until in subsequent visits to various stores, we nearly always found a parking space very close to the main store entrance. And it has continued to happen—virtually every time! Sometimes, as we approach, two or three drivers simultaneously back their cars out of choice parking spaces. Margaret and I smile and say: "Our Parking Angel is on the job again." Parking our car is a small matter, but can be a larger issue to people who do not walk well. We have learned to be grateful for even small blessings that come our way.

You may not see anything supernatural in this. You may even think that we have become delusional in our old age, or what we are seeing is merely wishful thinking or coincidental. You may possibly be right. But "we know that all things work together for good to them that love God" (Rom. 8:28). In other words, faith sees the invisible, believes the incredible, and receives the impossible! "Faith is the substance of things hoped for, the evidence of things not seen" (Heb. 11:1).

# CHAPTER EIGHT

## "Fern Is Dead!"

Shortly after I retired from the university faculty, late one night our telephone began to ring. We had just gone to sleep, but the phone rang with the kind of after-hours insistence that makes us think of possible family calamities. When I picked up the telephone receiver, I was temporarily assured to hear the voice of Lily, another retired faculty colleague. But Lily was clearly upset as she cried, "Fern is dying!" As I groggily tried to gather my wits and offer some words of comfort, Lily hung up on me. At that point, I was upset and phoned June, another female faculty member who also knew Lily. I asked June and her husband Jim, to meet me in front of Lily's apartment. We were not acquainted with Fern, but our mission was to offer condolences and assistance to Lily.

June recalled that Lily had two elderly sisters—Ivy and Violet—who lived in New England. We thought that Lily lived alone, but apparently she shared the apartment with a friend or companion. When we approached Lily's door, we saw that all the lights were on. After ringing the doorbell, a distraught and weeping Lily quickly invited us in. "Oh Fern!" she moaned as she led us into the bedroom. We were expecting the worst, but to our surprise the room was empty—except for the usual furniture. Puzzled, June asked, "Where is Fern?" And Lily motioned despairingly toward the window.

And then our bewildered eyes fell on a large potted plant—wilted and drooping—obviously in very serious condition. No joke! Our old friend's companion Fern was a houseplant—literally, a *fern*! As we took in the astonishing scene, Lily cried that she had always given Fern plenty of sunshine, water, and plant food—plus an occasional aspirin tablet. June was the first to recover from our surprise and moved to comfort Lily in her arms. Jim and I looked for Fern's pulse and considered CPR. There was no response, and I sadly pronounced, "I'm sorry, but Fern is dead."

I carefully removed the corpse in a large plastic bag, promising a dignified and respectful burial. Jim suggested replacing Lily's friend with new fern—a young sprout of the same plant family—appropriately waiting at a nearby nursery. I even thought we might try to transfer her affection from flora to fauna by getting Lily to adopt a young cat from the county animal shelter. She could name the cat Rose or Rosie. Finally, we adjourned our midnight wake for Fern with Lily going home with June and Jim for the rest of the night while I officiated at Fern's last rites in the alley by the garbage dumpster.

As I drove home, the events of the night got me to thinking: Before her retirement, Lily has been a bright, congenial, and well-balanced faculty member. She had never shown any overt signs of neurosis or aberrant behavior. After she left the university, we lost touch with Lily—assuming that she had adequate social support in friends, church, and community. Apparently, we were wrong in that assumption. Separated from her former profession, colleagues, and students, life became uninteresting and desperately lonely for Lily. In contrast to the confident, well-groomed professional we knew and admired just a year earlier, Lily now appeared gaunt and disheveled. Her personality became unusually introverted and colorless, as she partially disengaged from reality.

A few days later, June convinced Lily to make an appointment with a medical specialist for a general physical checkup. June accompanied her. We were pleased to learn that for a sixty-six-year-old, Lily was in reasonably good health. Her cognitive ability also appeared to be acceptable, but emotionally she suffered insomnia, loss of appetite, depression, and extreme loneliness.

At the physician's suggestion, June scheduled Lily for a series of appointments with a professional counselor. She responded very well to the counselor, who wryly reported to June that the situation could have been worse: "Rather than making friends with a houseplant, Lily might have identified herself as a fern." My imagination went wild as I briefly speculated about her possible use of fertilizer and pesticides! But happily, Lily was showing remarkable progress back from the brink of psychosis.

## A Sociological Explanation

More seriously, I recalled some research I had conducted several years earlier that confirmed the physician's observations regarding Lily's symptoms. Paradoxically, even in the midst of our crowded human society with frenetic social opportunities and excitement, loneliness is the most commonly cited social problem by Americans (Bynum 2011).

As a sociologist, I don't believe that Lily's fond attachment to a houseplant or any other object is as uncommon as we might assume. The world is full of solitary, lonely, and frightened individuals who are crying out and reaching out for someone—or something—to love and call their own. This is a normal human need. Our Creator was the first to identify the problem: "It is not good for man [or woman] to live alone" (Gen. 2:18 KJV).

Obviously, not all of our relationships are with other humans. It is normal and acceptable—and even encouraged—for infants and small children to adopt dolls, blankets, and other familiar objects as inseparable security companions. As children grow and experience the love of family and friends and develop socially, these inanimate objects are almost always discarded.

Living animal pets remain as highly valued companions to countless people. Association between humans and dogs (touted as man's best friend), cats, birds, horses—and even exotic lizards and other creatures—have often proved beneficial to the physical and emotional well-being of many people. Our local pet cemetery is a memorial to these meaningful human/animal relationships. However, *exclusive* association with animals is not a psychologically healthy substitute for members of the human race.

As I reviewed these possible options, I concluded that Lily's irrational personification of Fern—the plant—represented an unnatural and dangerous disengagement from people. Therefore, rehabilitating and reconnecting Lily with human society would *not* be served by replacing Fern with another plant, a pet rock, or even a cat named Rosie.

Admittedly, close association and involvement with human society always has some intrinsic hazards for everyone. We all run the risk of being vulnerable, exploited, manipulated, rejected, frightened, injured, and getting our hearts broken and feelings hurt by some people. On the other hand, the great majority of us willingly and eagerly throw ourselves into human society because those people with the potential to hurt us also have the potential to support and love us. They can fill our lives with friendship, companionship, joy, meaning, and purpose.

Considering our intrinsic need for these high-priority benefits of successful human interaction, our decision is really a no-brainer. Participation in human society is well worth the risk! In a minority of cases like Lily's, failure to satisfactorily fulfill one's social and spiritual needs through a rich experience with humanity is tragic and dangerous. Prolonged isolation (voluntarily or involuntarily) can lead to a state of social atrophy, boredom, and an empty, meaningless life.

## The Resuscitation of Lily

Fern was dead. So we focused our concern where it belonged—on the survival of Lily. A small coalition of her former associates at the university cautiously and purposefully set out to breathe new life into Lily and free her from the prison of solitude. Gradual and persistent efforts were made to get her out of that small and confining apartment and into the community. Shopping and entertainment excursions with pleasant companions slowly began to extricate Lily from her self-imposed exile. She looked forward to the fun and activities of these social contacts and challenges. Like a child learning to engage in social experiences, Lily gained confidence as she began to think of herself as a member of the group—in the collective and embracing terms of *we* and *us* and *our*— rather than in the narrow and restricting confines of *me, myself,* and *I.*

Lily began to bloom again as she participated in lively and stimulating conversations and activities with her newfound friends. She was no longer overly suspicious, fearful, negative, and downcast and took an active interest in other people. Tentatively at first, Lily became an active member of the local Retired Educators' Club. Through the years, Lily had become a nominal Christian and seldom visited a church. But now, on her own, she renewed her affiliation with the religious denomination of her youth. Lily wisely joined a small congregation in the suburbs—more conducive to informal primary group relationships than the large and more formal downtown church (Thompson and Hickey, 1999).

Over time, Lily regained her naturally outgoing personality. We were pleased when Lily volunteered to play the piano and teach a Sunday school class of children. She no longer focused her pity on herself and offered to assist in the charitable activities at a community welfare center. About a year later, my wife and I chanced to encounter Lily at a popular buffet luncheon. "How are you, Lily?" I asked. And my former colleague replied with an animated smile, "The fern is dead—but I am alive!"

# CHAPTER NINE

## The Truck Stop Shower

**B**efore I share this particular retirement experience with you, I must acknowledge that my many years in the campus "halls of ivy" imprinted me with the style and stereotype of the college professor. For example, I found that my occupational role and identity could not even be camouflaged by the anonymity of highway travel. In order to relieve the tedium of long and lonely automobile trips between my home near Oklahoma State University and occasional teaching and research assignments at other universities in the Midwest, I installed a two-way, citizen-band radio in my car. Then, with the CB manual in hand, I enthusiastically sallied forth on Interstate 35 to make friendly contact with equally-equipped fellow travelers. Most of the voices I heard on the airways belonged to truck drivers whose commercial eighteen-wheelers snorted impatiently up and down Interstate 35.

In preparation for this new social adventure, I gleaned from the CB manual a little of the official and homespun jargon used by the truckers. As a final preparatory step, I adopted as my citizen-band handle the innocuous moniker of Crackerjack, inspired by a nearby box of popcorn and my first name. Armed with these new communication tools, I confidently turned on my citizen-band radio and listened for a few minutes to the colorful chatter of truckers discussing weather and road conditions, the nearest Highway Patrol radar trap, and the quality of food at their next watering hole. Then I cheerily announced my presence: "Hello, good buddies! This is Crackerjack. What are road conditions on Interstate 35 South?"

Immediately, all the familiar, laid-back, citizen-band conversation stopped. I waited a minute before sending out my greeting and inquiry a second time. Finally, a surly voice answered with a deep southern drawl, "Where are you, Crackerjack?" Trying to sound cool and knowledgeable, I observed: "Just overtook Milepost Sixty-Two." At that, my newfound friend replied: "My road conditions are the same as yours. I'm in the fast lane right behind you." Quickly looking back, I was horrified to see a huge truck bearing down on my bumper—so fast and so close that the radiator seemed to fill up the rear window of my car. I had been so engrossed with my new CB toy, I had allowed my speed to drop down to fifty miles per hour, and the trucker behind me was clearly irritated.

On subsequent trips, I was a little more knowledgeable in making my citizen-band contacts. I managed to communicate effectively with Big Red, Wichita Kid, Ladies Man, and several other road regulars. They were cordial enough, but there was no real camaraderie. They didn't seem to fully accept me into their society, and I wondered if I had said something offensive. Perhaps I had the wrong inflection in my voice when I said "good buddy" or identified myself as Crackerjack. Maybe my vocabulary or sentence structure stigmatized me as an unacceptable outsider. Perhaps they detected a stuffy academic.

One night these suspicions were confirmed. Unobtrusively eavesdropping on the citizen-band channel, I heard two of the truck drivers mention me. "Have you heard from Crackerjack lately?" one asked. "Oh, you mean the Professor?" another voice responded. "Naw, I haven't heard him lately on the road." And a third trucker chimed in, "Maybe he doesn't drive I-35 anymore." I was surprised. Though I had never mentioned my occupation to any of them, apparently diction, or vocabulary, or message content had somehow given away my artificial role and pretense to be one like them. They rejected Crackerjack and gave me a more suitable citizen-band handle (Bynum 2011).

## The Flood of 1997

Those citizen-band conversations were my first exploratory contacts with truck drivers. Now, let's fast forward a few years into my Oregon retirement when a natural disaster accidently thrust me much deeper into the unique and fascinating trucker subculture.

In January of 1997, the city of Ashland, Oregon, experienced a sudden flood. A week of unusually warm rain prematurely melted much of the winter snowpack on the surrounding mountains. A massive runoff poured across the city's watershed (appropriately named!), roared down normally serene Ashland Creek through Lithia Park, flooded the plaza and many nearby shops with several feet of dirty water, and continued to the east down Water Street (appropriately named!).

In the process, the flood contaminated the city's source of drinking water whose supply lines reached as far as our home south of Ashland. For two weeks after the flood, Oregon National Guard trucks transported purified drinking water to central locations for thirsty citizens. While we had adequate drinking water during the emergency, there was no water for washing clothes or bathing. Under normal conditions, we take these services for granted. But as the water shortage turned from days into weeks, many people began to demonstrate an aromatic need and desire for a bath or shower. This circumstance led me to look outside our immediate, flood-stricken area for a solution.

## Country Lil's Super Truck Stop

I recalled buying gasoline several weeks earlier at Country Lil's truck stop about eight miles away on Interstate Five. At that time I noticed a large sign announcing that clean, private shower stalls were available to truck drivers for a nominal fee. Following a hunch that Country Lil was not dependent on the City of Ashland for water, I drove down the highway to the truck stop. I longed for a hot shower and was determined to get one somewhere, somehow.

First-class truck stops are equipped with oversized fuel islands and parking areas, a truck repair garage, snack/hardware/gift shop, game room, lounge, shower stalls, and a good restaurant—often featuring extra-large food servings and telephone/laptop computer connections in each booth. Country Lil even had a worn-out truck trailer chapel parked out back with a simple white cross painted on the door. It was informally staffed on weekends by one or two volunteer trucker-chaplains who offered free coffee, Christian fellowship, and a small gospel of John to any truck driver inclined to visit their chapel. Such truck stops are subcultural islands—generally inhabited by people one does not ordinarily find in my campus world of students and professors.

Most of the truck drivers I encountered were tired and quiet professionals, eager to get back on the road to their destinations. However, propelled by my quest for a hot shower, I chanced into a more rowdy subgroup of truckers in Country Lil's shower reservation line. I had naively brought with me my past experiences registering at professional academic meetings, which turned out to be a misperception of the truck stop situation.

We slowly worked our way up to a counter where each man registered his name and company affiliation and paid a six-dollar fee to a sleepy clerk in exchange for a small bar of soap, a towel, and a numbered card. Each man then took a seat in a large room to await his turn in a vacant shower stall. The waiting room contained about twenty truck drivers who proudly wore their diesel fumes and body odor without excuse— like the road warriors they are. My companions were noisily consuming hamburgers, pretzels, and beer around a huge television screen displaying wrestlers Earthquake Chaos and Bone- Crusher McGrudge maiming each other in the ring and wrecking tables and chairs outside the ring. I settled down in the crowd with a 7-Up soda, a couple of cookies, and a book, *The Scientific Method of Empirical Investigation*—guaranteed to cure insomnia.

From time to time, a male attendant would stick his head into the room and call for the next shower registrant. For example, "Rocky Hammer: Acme Concrete and Stone Construction. Shower number twelve." In response, a rough and tough-talking character grunted and swaggered down the hallway toward the showers. At that point, I had my first suspicion that I didn't fit in very well with my companions in Country Lil's shower waiting room. I felt like the classic out-of-place

Marginal Man described by sociologist Everett Stonequist—"the uninvited, unwelcome, and uncomfortable misfit in an established social group" (1937).

The next shower call was for "Tank Sharkey: U.S. Steel Freight Haulers. Shower number five." And a three-hundred--pound incredible hulk with a shaved head and a tattooed serpent coiled up his right arm shook the floor as he headed for the showers.

As I viewed the unfolding spectacle and began scribbling out my impressions, the attendant again arrived at the doorway. And all conversation stopped and every head turned to curiously look around the room as he made his next shower call: "Professor J. E. Bynum: Southern Oregon University. Shower number ten." No one responded or moved toward the showers, even to a second call. Finally, glancing briefly in my direction, the attendant inquired, "Are you Professor Bynum?"

Lowering my voice an octave to a raspy croak, I facetiously stammered, "I'm Paul Bunyan with the Grizzly Mountain Logging Company." Some laughter from the truckers indicated that they caught on to my joke—and caught on to my uncomfortable pretense. At that, the next name was called and shower number ten went to Buster Doberman of Ace Cross-Country Trucking, who headed for the showers. I don't know what became of Professor Bynum because I soon gathered up my book, 7-Up can, and these notes and left the truck stop.

NOTE: The reader should not interpret the above anecdote as a disparagement of the truckers. On the contrary, while I felt uncomfortable and out-of-place in the unaccustomed circumstances, I must confess that the truck drivers were more genuine and forthright in their role than I was in mine.

# CHAPTER TEN

## The Southpaw

I gave away my old baseball glove last week—not because I am too old to effectively play the game anymore—though that is true. Nor is that worn, leather glove a symbol of unfulfilled dreams of what might have been—though it is small leftover of adolescent excitement on the baseball diamond. Neither of these speculations can explain my motive. I gave the old baseball glove away because an old man is looking to the future. So indulge me a few minutes to tell the story of a left-hander in a right-handed world.

~

I was born over eighty years ago. And when I was a young child, people began to perceive me as different—with a personal physical anomaly that set me apart from other children. As a youngster, I demonstrated a decided tendency to favor my left hand over my right hand in eating and playing. Relatives and neighbors noticed my developing left-handedness and exchanged hopeful projections: "Oh, it is only temporary and irrelevant in young children" or, "The child will outgrow it in time and settle into the 'normal' and 'acceptable' right-handed behavior."

Historically, left-handed people often faced serious discrimination in many societies. For instance, during the European Middle Ages (5 to 15 centuries AD), members of this highly visible minority were stigmatized as unlucky, deviant, and even sinister—possibly possessed by evil spirits. The superstitious maxim prevailed that "Right is right and left is wrong!" Consequently, about twelve percent of the population was assigned an aberrant, marginal social status.

However, by the dawn of the twentieth century, the first medical and educational research on handedness suggested that the cause of left-hand dominance in some individuals is neurological rather than a stubborn bad habit or spiritual disorder. Favoring the left hand began to be understood as the natural and normal condition for some individuals. In addition, evidence began to accumulate that attempts to force left-handed children to comply with right-handed social expectations could result in serious side-effects in childhood development, such as disrupting normal patterns of speech. Slowly, the intolerant rejection of left-handedness began to soften and subside (Wikipedia 2012).

During the 1930s, as I persisted in my deviant childhood preference for the left hand, my parents made a few futile attempts to train, bribe, or cajole me into using my right hand in a more dominant way. They soon abandoned their efforts. Aside from this minor family concern, I was a happy and healthy young boy. I loved my teachers and classmates in elementary school, and I was a good student—especially in reading, spelling, and basic arithmetic. But soon my nonconforming left-handedness received broader attention. There were still some educators who insisted that the small minority of children favoring the left hand should be encouraged to change their orientation to the right hand in order to socially survive in a right-handed world.

I encountered that rigid position when elementary school teachers began teaching me to write. There were no convenient ballpoint pens in those days, so penmanship was standardized and straightforward. Every young student was instructed to grasp a metal pen in his or her right hand, dip the point in black liquid ink, and transcribe the printed or cursive letters and words from left to right across a writing tablet—leaving the finished product clearly and cleanly behind the right-moving hand and pen.

On the other hand (no pun intended), a left-hander—in transcribing his freshly written work from left to right on the tablet—trailed the written word with his left hand, ending each sentence with fresh ink smudged across the paper and on the offending hand. (No wonder teachers were dismayed over the resulting mess!) The instructor's demand for a right-handed approach to my early penmanship exercises quickly led to a confrontation with my mother, who insightfully insisted that I must be taught to write and allowed to develop my own style.

So we proceeded with me making a choice between two accommodations available to left-handed writers. First, I could learn to write with the left hand held straight and extending the pen *below* the emerging line of script. This position would likely produce a slanting backhand line of occasionally overlapping letters—but safely below the advancing left hand as it moves to the right.

I choose the second option. I learned to write with my left forearm and hand holding the pen, crooked *above* the emerging line of script— thus avoiding the unsightly blotting of freshly inked words. This awkward-looking writing style does not generally produce attractive script, but it enabled me to remain left-handed while becoming literate and avoiding the original untidy, ink-blotting alternative.

While that brief elementary school conflict over my early writing attempts reached a compromise and quick resolution between teacher and parent, it initiated and prepared me for a lifetime of struggle to satisfactorily adapt my left-handedness to the demands of a right-handed world (Rutledge and Donley 1992). I customarily sat a little sideways in classroom chairs constructed with writing surfaces on the right side. I often encountered and learned to use tools, can openers, musical instruments, cameras, computer keyboards, etc., designed and mass-produced for the large right-handed market. Even the customer courtesy pen—attached by a short, lightweight chain at my bank cashier's window—is mounted on my right side. This arrangement can entangle a left-handed client. Over time, lefties become resourceful and adapt to such inconveniences.

When I was a young man preparing to leave home for a military enlistment, my mother taught me a few simple sewing techniques such as reattaching buttons and mending socks. Then she presented me with a pair of left-handed scissors. Later, I took those basic sewing skills and special scissors with me into dormitory life on a college campus. I still have those left-handed scissors as a fond memory of my mother's wisdom and foresight in preparing me to function in a right-handed world.

Through the years, researchers from many academic disciplines continue to be fascinated by left-handedness—often claiming such inane and questionable minutia as "left-handed people tend to chew their food on the right side of the mouth!"

I wish that I could report some noteworthy accomplishment in my life that ultimately overcame all social intolerance of my deviant and distracting left-handedness. For examples, "Lefty" Michelangelo painted his unforgettable masterpiece on the ceiling of the Sistine Chapel. "Lefty" Joan of Arc turned military defeat into victory for France. And five of seven recent presidents of the United States defied statistical probability by being left-handed (DeKay and Huffaker 1985). But I labored in vain to turn my handicap into full social acceptance. That is—except for one brief and shining moment of unexpected public appreciation for my left-handed proclivity.

It was the beginning of my freshman year in a Texas high school. In response to a desperate search by our coach for potential athletic ability in our small school, many male students participated in perfunctory tryouts for the baseball team. I will never forget the moment when I was handed a baseball and told to throw it toward home plate where a large hero from the previous year's team was routinely smashing the feeble student offerings over the fence. My only experience with a baseball was occasionally playing backyard catch with my brother and cousins. So my first pitch failed to reach home plate. My second effort nearly hit the batter. Then, to everyone's surprise, the hulking slugger flailed helplessly at my next three pitches and struck out.

I was the most surprised of all. Amazingly, my well-known left-handed affliction—when translated into an unfamiliar pitching stance and awkward windup—had endowed me with just two pitches: a wild, erratic throw and a natural, sharp-breaking curve. Somehow that combination baffled enough right-handed hitters to earn a place for me among the relief pitchers on our struggling high school baseball team. I was a southpaw—a slang expression for left-handed pitchers dating back to at least 1885. Most baseball diamonds are laid out with home plate to the west. This arrangement results in the left-handed pitcher facing south before delivering the ball to his catcher behind home plate. Hence, the left-handed pitcher was called a southpaw. Our coach concluded that my unpredictable wild pitch served to set up some nervous hitters for the effective curve that followed.

Socially, my left-handedness was no longer seen as an unfortunate and inferior aberration. On the contrary, it became a source of positive attention and celebration in our small community. But my newfound identify and appreciation was only temporary. My high school baseball exploits lasted less than a year—cut short by football injuries involving a sprained left shoulder and broken collarbone.

As the decades passed, I learned to accommodate my left-handedness to the never-ending challenges of a right-handed world. Ultimately, I became a university professor and spent nearly forty years with young people in a rewarding teaching career. However, I still occasionally find myself tying a reverse, left-handed version of the Windsor knot on my necktie; or casually scanning and reading a magazine from back to front. These little mannerisms are not illegal—just different from the way most people handle neckties and magazines. I don't need to explain or excuse such unusual behaviorisms. It's just the way my left-handed brain functions. And if it works for me, social approval is not necessary.

My wife, two children, and six grandchildren are unanimously right-handed. However, I believe that somewhere in my genetic blueprint lurks an obscure, recessive, left-handed gene. It may suddenly appear again down my hereditary line. So I have bequeathed my old, left-hander's baseball glove to my descendants with the admonition to carefully look for a future family member who shows signs of developing a dominant left hand. That fortunate child is to receive my old baseball glove with the pronouncement: "You are special! You are Great-Grandpa's Southpaw! You too can overcome the challenges in the game of life." Or, as veteran baseball catchers often welcome rookie pitchers entering the game, "*Go get 'em, Kid!*" (Uecker 1982).

# CHAPTER ELEVEN

## Does God Have a Sense of Humor?

The title of this chapter is a rhetorical question to introduce a profound and abstract topic. That is, this question is posed as we consider the mind and purposes of God. The question may not have a completely satisfying answer because if human beings could fully fathom God's personality and mental processes, He would not be big enough to be God. "Can you search out the deep things of God Can you find out the limits of the Almighty? They are higher than heaven—what can you do? Deeper than Sheol—what can you know? Their measure is longer than the earth and broader than the sea" (Job 11:7–9 NKJV).

Does God have a sense of humor? The question exposes our own cognitive limitations. We must be careful that the question does not suggest an audacious and irreverent attempt to impute human characteristics to the Creator. He is the unlimited, divine pattern; and finite man is the earthly product. The master plan is that eventually faith, love, peace, and other qualities of God's character will be perfectly reflected in us. That is—by beholding the Lord's divine example and following His way—we become forever changed to be like Him.

With that acknowledgement being said—I am a consummate people watcher. During my retirement years, I have turned my sociological focus on the behavior of people in a religious context. This chapter is comprised of serendipitous observations and indications of God's subtle humor in His interactions with humans.

## The Witch

Citizens of the United States are blessed with the Constitutionally-guaranteed right to accept or reject religious beliefs and practices. This freedom of religion has resulted in a wide assortment of religious persuasions. In addition to the more traditional and prominent Judeo-Christian variations entrenched in the culture of the larger American society, a wide spectrum of uncommon religious sects and cults also make their presence known.

For instance, just before retiring from my last teaching appointment, I was approached by an unusual student enrolled in my Social Problems course. She was in her mid-thirties with piercing eyes, uncut hair to her waist, and dressed in an unconventional robe. She introduced herself as a witch and a priestess who serves at the altar of a local Wicca coven (religious group). The name *Wicca* is a contraction based on their practice of witchcraft and black magic.

The cult's ancient worship rituals focus on basic dimensions of the physical universe identified as air, fire, water, and earth. Although Wiccans deny that they are Satanists, their spiritual focus on nature and an amoral rejection of a central deity or authority seem pagan and pantheistic at least. I was relieved to learn—contrary to an unverified rumor—that Wicca rituals do *not* include human sacrifices.

My new student did alert me that she was subject to sudden trancelike states followed by out-of-body experiences. "On two occasions," I was informed, "[she] had been found in the tops of large, virtually inaccessible trees—under the influence of her religion" (or whatever hallucinating potion she was taking). As I considered these prospects, I realized that the chances of an exciting, out-of-mind semester were high. As a veteran university teacher, I had been confronted by students exhibiting drunkenness, violence, medical problems, childbirth, stalking behavior, and sophisticated cheating—but this classroom interaction with a self-proclaimed witch promised to be a new challenge. We proceeded through the course with several humorous and good-natured exchanges between us. We mostly debated the requirement that "instructors and students must be present and functional in both body and mind for on-campus classes." Happily, there were no unwelcome or frightening incidents.

Her presence reminded me of the tolerance for religious diversity guaranteed by the Constitution of the United States. Such diversity can not only broaden our knowledge of alternative religious beliefs and practices, but stimulate the learning environment. The exposure to unique people and perspectives can help to open our minds to objective, comparative analysis and confirm our own religious beliefs.

## Humor in the Bible

There is considerable biblical evidence that humorous satire, puns, riddles, irony, and delightful anecdotes are liberally included in the divinely-inspired Old and New Testaments (Friedman and Stern, 2000). Here are a few of the examples:

(1) Abraham, the "Father of the Hebrew nation," and Sarah, his wife, shared a lively sense of humor—even regarding a prophetic message from God: "And he [the messenger] said to [Abraham], 'Where is Sarah your wife?' So he said, 'Here in the tent.' And He said, 'I will certainly return to you according to the time of life. And behold, Sarah your wife shall have a son' .... Now Abraham and Sarah were old, well advanced in age, and Sarah had passed the age of childbearing. Therefore Sarah laughed within herself, saying, 'After I have grown old, shall I have pleasure, and my lord [Abraham] is also old?'"(Gen. 18:9–12 NKJV).

On the same subject, Hebrews 11:12 may be the funniest verse in the Bible: "Therefore there was born even of [Abraham], and him as good as dead at that, as many descendants as the stars of heaven ...(NASB).

(2) In the book of Jonah, we read that God instructed the prophet Jonah to warn the inhabitants of the city of Nineveh of impending judgments for their gross sins. But Jonah tried to get out of the responsibility and took passage on a ship sailing the other way from Nineveh. However, God intercepted the runaway prophet with a three-day ride in the belly of a huge fish. One can imagine—with a smile—how Jonah must have looked and smelled when the fish vomited him back

onto dry land before Jonah headed for Nineveh with his remarkable fish story and the prophetic warning from God (Jonah 1 and 2 NKJV).

Later, after God rescued Nineveh, Jonah threw a temper tantrum about a vine dying and how he was hot and uncomfortable without the shade: "*I am mad enough to die!*" (Jonah 4:8, Reardon 2010).

(3) Balaam was another stubborn prophet who ignored God's instructions. His story is also recorded in the Old Testament when a nearby king starts to worry as he sees the Israelites growing in numbers and spreading out. King Balak is afraid that they will eventually invade and conquer his territory of Moab. So he contacts Balaam—a minor Hebrew prophet who seemed to be one who could deliver a curse on Israel for a rich gift of silver. They make the deal, and Balaam saddles his donkey and rides off toward the Israeli encampment.

Three times Balaam tried to curse Israel, but God intervened, and the only words that came out of Balaam's mouth were beautiful blessings on Israel. On the last trip to deliver his curse and collect the money, Balaam and his donkey were going through a very narrow gorge in the mountains. Suddenly a shining angel carrying a large sword appeared just ahead on the trail. Balaam did not see the angel, but the donkey did and stopped in his tracks. Balaam hit the stubborn donkey, who finally struggles ahead on the narrow trail—scraping Balaam's foot painfully against the sharp and rocky wall. Again, Balaam beats the poor donkey that had much better spiritual eyesight than his master.

At that point, God allowed the donkey to speak and give the first recorded statement against cruelty to animals. Then the Lord opened Balaam's eyes so he too saw the powerful angel blocking the trail, who rebuked the unfaithful and mercenary prophet for conspiring against the Israelites. While Balaam had been unable to speak his intended curse, by contrast, God gave voice to a humble animal. Apparently, Balaam was not surprised by his conversation with a donkey. But think how ludicrous and comical Balaam must have looked and sounded when he later reported the incident (Num. 22).

(4) Although Jesus had the most serious role and task in human history and never forgot to give the highest priority to "His Father's business" (Luke 2:49), there is abundant documentation that He had a

well-balanced, social personality and loved to interact informally with individuals, groups, and crowds of people. His parables or stories were often sprinkled with humorous word play, satire, and hyperbole. Some scholars contend that if we could place the utterances of Jesus in the language and cultural context of His time and place, we could see that Jesus often regaled and delighted his audiences (Martin 2011).

An example is His parable about the rich man who died and went to heaven, where he rested his head on Abraham's bosom. Another story compares the possibility of a rich man getting into heaven to a camel passing through the eye of a needle. These witty and outlandish illustrations must have attracted and charmed Jesus' listeners as they visualized the humorous descriptions of "Abraham's bosom" and "a camel in the eye of a needle" before catching on to the spiritual interpretations and applications (Luke 16:22; 18:25).

## Contemporary Humor in God's House

One does not have to look long and hard to see spontaneous and humorous events in the Christian churches of various denominations. Through the years, my wife and I were present when many small incidents evoked a combination of smiles and empathy from observers. For instance, Margaret was a member of a church choir when an unforgettable wardrobe malfunction occurred. A distinguished lady was vigorously directing the choir in Handel's classic "See the Conquering Hero Comes" when her half-slip suddenly slipped down under her skirt and into public view around her ankles. There were a few gasps from witnesses, but the choir bravely pressed on. However, the unflappable choir director was the one who really saved the situation. Without missing a beat, she calmly stepped out of the fallen slip and completed the victorious anthem. She smiled and bowed to the applauding audience before retrieving her fallen slip and resumed the concert. What class!

A more difficult situation to remedy occurred in a multi-purpose college auditorium used for secular performances during the week and religious services on weekends. An informal evening rehearsal for a forthcoming secular play was held in the auditorium when soft drinks were consumed by the actors. Apparently, a can of acidic soda was spilled in the seat of a wooden chair. Unknown to the actors present and the participants the next day in the religious service, the invisible soda transformed the wood varnish on the chair seat into the consistency and power of Super Glue.

As the subsequent religious service commenced the next morning, the college chaplain and other religious dignitaries reverently filed in and were seated on the rostrum. Words can hardly describe the embarrassing spectacle when the organist began to play and everyone stood to sing the hymn: "Just as I Am, I Come to Thee." A church officer found himself firmly glued to his chair. Rather than ripping the seat out of the chair or his trousers, he stood in that awkward situation during the opening hymn and prayer. Witnesses recall how difficult it was to regain the dignity and decorum of the religious service with a chair glued to someone's posterior.

## The Church of the Open Door

Another humorous incident occurred during a recent Sunday morning service at The Church of the Open Door. It was reported that a big, intimidating, and uninvited dog casually ambled into a church service one Sunday morning. After a few sniffs of startled worshippers, the unescorted beast calmly hopped into a back pew to observe the ongoing religious service. The flustered minister manfully tried to stay with his sermon on "Welcoming the Stranger in Our Midst." However, the distraction of the large dog seated on a back pew demanded the congregation's attention. Pausing in his homily, the pastor called upon the deacons to remove the dog from the church.

As the uncertain deacons approached the large animal, they paused in the aisle where a wry old deacon with a twinkle in his eye turned to the pastor for fresh instructions: "Pardon the interruption, Pastor, but the creature has unusual credentials to remain in God's house." The now irritated minister replied: "What do you mean? Please remove the dog!" But the deacon held his ground: "Pastor, the animal is a saint!" The minister wondered if his deacon had lost his mind and asked incredulously: "A saint, you say?" And he sarcastically added: "And what saint is he?" The congregation seated near the great dog gave way to uncontrolled laughter as the deacon responded: "Saint Bernard!"

## Long-Winded Preachers

We have learned from long-suffering experience that while some marathon sermons are forgotten over time, the memory of long-winded preachers may last forever. A while back, Margaret and I were seated in church as a visiting preacher droned on in a two-hour-long sermon. He was much more than your typical, long-winded clergyman. Without doubt, the speaker felt divinely called to exhaust his subject and his hearers with every remote detail and slight nuance of his favorite topic. For our part—many of those present were convinced that this preacher could break the endurance record of even the most devout congregations.

He reminded me of the New Testament account of Eutychus, who fell asleep during a long, loong, looong all-night sermon by the apostle Paul. When the sleeping youth fell out of an upper window and was apparently killed by the fall, the apostle was equal to the emergency. Paul paused in his sermon just long enough to revive the youth before resuming his discourse until morning (Acts 20:7–11). And the thought crossed my mind: *I hope that our preacher can also raise the dead!*

On another occasion, we attended a church located across the street from a fire truck factory. Every day, an infamous, overwhelming, noontime whistle from the factory reminded everyone that someday a trumpet blast from heaven will indeed raise the dead. On the Sabbath in question, we were patiently waiting for a visiting dignitary to terminate his lengthy sermon "The Judgment Day." At twelve o'clock sharp, when the deafening factory whistle sounded across the street, church members knowingly glanced at each other and whispered: "That twelve noon blast is our hope for a dismissal from church. It has worked before to save us from long-winded preachers." But our present speaker didn't flinch or pause (though he had already been preaching for well over an hour). He was firm in his conviction that he was under holy orders and continued his sermon. Our hope had been dashed—replaced by the speaker's reference to an agonizing line from Dante's *Inferno*: "Abandon hope all ye who enter here!"

About 12:45 p.m., a few exhausted people staggered out to take their prescribed medications or to visit the rest rooms. The ladies in charge of the potluck luncheon excused themselves to dutifully check on their aging casseroles. Then—at about one, a new and astonishing message came to the preacher. A large clock—mounted on the back wall and facing the rostrum—mysteriously fell off the wall with a startling crash. The disabled clock hung by a two-foot long electrical cord, with its' face turned to the wall. The speaker stopped in mid-sentence and thoughtfully gazed out over the remaining survivors of his marathon sermon. He glanced at his pocket watch and considered aloud the possibility that the deacons had somehow sabotaged his sermon by disabling the wall clock. More seriously, he pondered the possibility that the falling clock might be a signal from God to make a reluctant end to his much speaking (Matt. 6:7). And we who witnessed his struggle unanimously agreed that God was directing his closure and silently thanked the Lord for rescue in our time of need!

## The Holy Kiss

Margaret and I observed this final example of unintended church-related humor at a recent funeral. Before you question the illogical connection between humor and death, I need to explain the unusual behavior of mourners at a funeral that appeared risky, peculiar, and even funny to outsiders. (Or perhaps the unusual behavior was *our* reaction to the mourners!)

For several years we had been acquainted with Frank and Edith, an elderly married couple in our hometown. We often enjoyed short and pleasant visits when we discussed our common interests in yard work, grandchildren, and local news events. Then Frank's health began to fail, and we were saddened when Edith reported that he had passed away. She invited us to the funeral/memorial service to be held at their church on the next Sunday afternoon. At the appointed hour, Margaret and I arrived early and were cordially ushered into a back pew. As we watched the church members arrive, we immediately realized that we were outside visitors to a different religious subculture.

Our old-fashioned and conservative sensibilities were startled by the inordinate amount of unrestrained kissing as church members greeted one another—only restricted to same-sex adults. Then it dawned upon me that we were witnessing a mass demonstration of the holy kiss—a distinctive religious ordinance still practiced by several small, Anabaptist sects. From our uninitiated point of view, all that enthusiastic and extracurricular smooching in the church aisle seemed like an overzealous feeding frenzy among sharks.

The tradition of greeting the brethren with a holy kiss (also referred to as the kiss of peace) is based on references at the ends of several letters from Paul and Peter to some of the churches they had earlier founded. Rather than enjoining the churches in general to practice the holy kiss of greeting, it is clear from the original language and context that the biblical writers were identifying just a few especially close friends to receive their apostolic greeting with a holy kiss. Nevertheless, a few small religious groups insist that the holy kiss is based upon apostolic authority and persist in the practice as a neglected ordinance of the Christian church (Ditzel 2010).

Today, the handshake prevails as a proper greeting in most English-speaking cultures. This gesture of Christian friendship and fellowship has also been traced back to the early apostles. For example, after Paul was converted to Christianity at Damascus, he and his companions traveled to Jerusalem to meet with leaders of the church: "And James, Peter, and John ... gave to me and Barnabas the right hands of fellowship" (Gal. 2:9).

But this historic review of the holy kiss and the fraternal handshake did nothing to alleviate our dilemma as visitors to our neighbors' church. Our anxiety was heightened during the testimonial portion of the service, when various members volunteered their spiritual experiences with Brother Frank. One elderly lady in particular caught our attention with a kiss and tell announcement: "Brother Frank," she giggled like a teenaged school girl, "gave me a holy kiss three times!" And I muttered to myself, "Frank--you old rascal!" After that, Margaret and I thought we detected several church members eyeing and smiling in our direction with Christian charity. (Many Christians have been suspicious of such behavior ever since Judas Iscariot utilized a kiss of greeting to signal his betrayal of Jesus [Luke 21:47]).

I gave some serious statistical thought to what was happening all around us before turning to my wife with a conclusion: "Margaret—the probability of us receiving some random kisses is all a matter of arithmetic. There are about one hundred adults in this crowd—equally divided between males and females. The chances are that each of us could receive up to fifty uninvited kisses within the next hour."

At that point, we began planning our exit strategy combined with an effort to make ourselves less kissable. I asked Margaret if she still had the medical face mask in her purse that she had worn at the Seattle Airport [See Chapter 3]. "Yes," she answered. "That might be my barrier against unwanted kissing. But Jack—what will you do?" It was time for an imaginative defense maneuver.

In my desperation to avoid becoming kissing cousins and the focus of unwanted brotherly affection, I recalled the clever ruse used by King David on one occasion in escaping a dangerous and uncomfortable situation: "And David changed his behavior before them, and feigned himself mad, and scrabbled on the doors, and let his spittle fall down upon his beard. Then said Achish unto his servants, Lo, ye see the man is mad: wherefore have ye brought him to me? David therefore departed thence, and escaped to the cave Adullam (1 Sam. 21:13–22:1). I suggested to Margaret that I cross my eyes, scratch the pew with my fingernails, emit incoherent vocal jabber, and drool a lot as she in her face mask led me out to the parking lot. "The impact might even cause them to revise their holy kiss theology," I whispered hopefully.

It was then that a new and disturbing thought crossed our minds: "It would be embarrassing to be approached by strangers who want to kiss us. On the other hand, it would be a terrible blow to our self-esteem to realize that we are so ugly and undesirable that nobody would want to kiss us." As Frank's funeral/memorial ended, all our concern turned out to be unnecessary. The church pastor and congregation were hospitable and discrete as they shook our hands and respectfully invited us back. And we carried home a profound lesson in tolerance for other people who have harmless beliefs and customs that significantly differ from ours.

## A Conclusion: Does God Have a Sense of Humor?

Yes, He does! But just as what a person considers humorous is determined by the cultural definitions prevalent in his or her society, so God's humor reflects the values and standards of heaven. Consequently, God's humor is more subtle and sophisticated than ours. The available biblical evidence of His occasional humorous satire, puns, parables, and anecdotes always have a spiritual point or lesson, and are never crude or cruel, rude or lewd.

It is clear that God perceives humor as an intrinsic part of the human social experience. Wise King Solomon—speaking and writing under divine guidance—brilliantly summarized the unfolding and balanced life course of man:

> "To everything there is a season;
> A time for every purpose under heaven:
> A time to be born, and a time to die;
> A time to plant, And a time to pluck what is planted;
> A time to kill, And a time to heal;
> A time to break down, And a time to build up;
> *A time to weep, And a time to laugh;*
> A time to mourn, and a time to dance;
> A time to cast away stones, And a time to gather stones;
> A time to embrace, And a time to refrain from embracing;
> A time to gain, And a time to lose;
> A time to keep, And a time to throw away;
> A time to tear, And a time to sew;
> A time to keep silence, And a time to speak;
> A time to love, And a time to hate;
> A time of war, And a time of peace."
> (Eccl. 3:1–8 NKJV, Italics supplied)

Thus, Solomon has contributed an answer to the question regarding God's sense of humor: "There is a time to weep, and a time to laugh!" Medical authorities agree that "laughter is good for your health by relaxing the whole body, boosting the immune system, help protect the heart, and stay emotionally healthy" (McGhee 2013). A good sense of humor—including the ability to laugh at ourselves—can enable us to roll with the punches and survive the setbacks and sorrows of life.

"A joyful heart is good medicine, but a broken spirit dries up the bones" (Prov. 17:22 HCSB). Laughter is medicine for the soul, but sometimes amid stresses of the day, we forget to take our medicine. Instead of viewing our world with a healthy mixture of optimism and cheerfulness, we allow worries and distractions to rob us of the joy that God intends for our lives.

Undoubtedly, every human will encounter events and circumstances of sorrow and trouble. At the same time, as many of the stories in this book illustrate, the human life course is also generously seasoned with happy endings and surprisingly humorous incidents. We must keep our eyes and ears and minds open to catch these rainbows in the midst of the storms.

So as we go about our daily activities, let us approach life with a smile on our lips and hope in our hearts. And laugh every chance we get. After all, God created laughter for a reason—and our heavenly Father knows best—so laugh!

# CHAPTER TWELVE

## Remember The Alamo
## (A Survivor's Report)

**"C**owboy Mac" McHugh and I go way back—all the way to our elementary school friendship in San Antonio, Texas. After our freshman year in high school, my family moved to California, and Mac's family moved to a cattle ranch in the Texas panhandle—from which Cowboy Mac acquired his nickname. Twenty-seven years later—after I joined the faculty at Oklahoma State University—Mac and I reconnected.

Twenty-five more years passed and the old professor and the old cowboy were getting gray, long in the tooth, and approaching retirement. So Cowboy Mac saddled up his Ford Mustang and rode to Stillwater for a last visit. As we exchanged colorful stories about our lives in transition, Mac shared the following anecdote. It is so appropriate for this book on retirement reorientation that with Mac's permission, I have shortened and reorganized his "last stand at the Alamo" and reported it below in Mac's own first personal pronouns of *I* and *me*, just as he orally communicated it to the author of this book.

In preparation for my retirement, I went over to Amarillo for my annual medical examination at the office of old Doc Kimball—my long-time primary physician. In the midst of our routine review of major world events and my occasional sciatica backache, Dr. Kimball casually interjected that some of my new and vague physical symptoms could indicate a common abdominal infection. Eager to demonstrate my own medical knowledge, I asked: "Doesn't that condition generally respond favorably to antibiotics?" Dr. Kimball agreed, but added, "First, I want to refer you to Dr. John Bowie at a nearby urology clinic for consultation and any necessary tests. I'll telephone ahead and set up your appointment."

At the mention of Dr. Bowie's name, my thoughts immediately went back to my childhood in San Antonio, Texas, and several spellbinding visits to the Alamo—the old Spanish mission where James Bowie, Davy Crocket, and a brave garrison of volunteers sacrificed their lives in a battle for Texas independence from Mexico. Colonel Jim Bowie's fame lives on in a namesake—the large and intimidating Bowie Frontier knife. *"Remember the Alamo!"* later became the Texans' battle cry as Sam Houston led them to the final victory for Texas independence.

With that historic and heroic saga in mind, I looked forward to meeting Dr. Bowie, and soon my wife and I were seated expectantly in his medical waiting room. When my name was called, I was greeted by a smiling, middle-aged woman. "I am Frieda, Dr. Bowie's nurse. Please follow me down the hall." Reassuringly, she gently touched my arm as we entered a small examination room and added, "Dr. Bowie will be along in a few minutes after we prepare for your scheduled cystoscopy." Her enthusiasm sounded like I was about to receive the Pulitzer Prize. "My cystoscopy?" I asked. "What is that?" Nurse Frieda continued in her patronizing manner, "We want to take some pictures of your bladder, Honey."

For a fleeting moment—still caught up in my boyish reverie about intrepid Colonel Jim Bowie at the Alamo—I wondered if I had chanced upon the cutting edge of medical science.

*"Wow!"* I thought. *"A photograph to commemorate this occasion— maybe of me standing between Dr. Bowie and Nurse Frieda!"* As my imagination ran wild, I told myself: *"I must remember to smile and stand up*

straight. *This picture could have an honored place in my photograph album at home—maybe even appear on our family Christmas card!*"

However, a new reality quickly took over when Nurse Frieda patted my shoulder and announced: "Take off your clothes in this cubicle, put on this hospital gown, and return to the examination room." Anyone familiar with a hospital gown never forgets that the gown is a thin, obscene garment with lots of southern exposure. And a confusing concern crossed my mind: *"They have confiscated my clothes. What is going on here? I'm glad that my wife is nearby in the waiting room."*

By now I was gaining a much fuller revelation regarding the nature and purpose of the cystoscopy examination. As astonishing as it sounds, Nurse Frieda was saying that a small camera would be inserted into my body with which Dr. Bowie would explore my insides for a suspected urinary infection. If such a condition was confirmed by his widescreen, Technicolor pictures (possibly shown in local theaters), I would receive appropriate antibiotic treatment. At this insight, I seriously considered the proposition that I might forgo the pending cystoscopy adventure because I could easily tolerate my symptoms for at least another year or so. Stretching a bit off the examination table where I reclined, I quickly double-checked Dr. John Bowie's medical credentials, conspicuously framed on a nearby wall. Then Dr. Bowie himself entered the examination room attired in his surgical scrubs and rubber gloves. I was relieved that he did not look like the fierce frontiersman, Jim Bowie of Alamo fame, the one with the big knife.

I regret that I cannot report that my cystoscopy examination was painless and uneventful, perhaps even edifying and inspiring, as I became the subject and the object of marvelous medical technology. With all due respect, Dr. Bowie and Nurse Frieda remained optimistic and committed to their Hippocratic Oath throughout the procedure. As for me, I had another bad moment when I caught a glimpse of the camera that was to be inserted into my body. It was actually very small, but from my perspective, it appeared to be about the same size as my old seven-pound camcorder. This estimate led to a rather testy verbal exchange between me and Nurse Frieda regarding pain control:

Cowboy Mac: "That camera could hurt a lot."

Nurse Frieda: "You will be moderately sedated to block most discomfort."

Cowboy Mac: "The sedation agent isn't working."

Nurse Frieda: "How can you know that? We haven't begun the procedure yet."

Cowboy Mac: "I can still hear your voice. I want you to use a stun gun on me—like they mercifully use on cattle going to the slaughter house."

Nurse Frieda thought I was joking and said: "Relax, Honey. It will be over in just a few minutes."

In general, I am pleased with my resolve during my Alamo-like experience. Although the cystoscopy is ranked on the fear scale right up there with dental root canal and just below the tortures of the Spanish Inquisition, I managed to control my impulse to hit Nurse Frieda and run in my hospital gown back to the safety of my wife and the crowd in the waiting room.

Finally, after I was fully aroused from the sedation, Dr. Bowie shook my hand as he proudly announced his discovery of a minor infection and prescribed a course of antibiotics for me. Nurse Frieda cheerfully said: "Good-bye, Honey." I retrieved my clothes and dignity and left the clinic knowing that I would always "Remember the Alamo."

~

Author's Note: In granting permission to include his massacre at the Alamo experience in this book, Cowboy Mac requested that his true name identity be covered by a pseudonym. He wanted to avoid the jocular comments of his ranch and rodeo associates. I have complied with that request.

# CHAPTER THIRTEEN

## Bedside Manners

It was two o'clock in the afternoon and visiting hours were just beginning at the hospital where my wife was recovering from surgery. Together, we had often visited relatives, friends, and neighbors who were hospital patients. Now the situation was reversed. We were to be on the receiving end of well-wishers and visitors. It took just one day for us to modify our belief in the commonly held view that hospital visiting hours are a vital, therapeutic part of the healing process. "Lord, save us from our friends!" soon became a daily prayer.

Finally, the physician ordered a sign placed on the door to my wife's room. Her illness was neither contagious nor critical. However, without that sign, rest and recuperation could not be achieved. The sign read simply: NO VISITORS. As we looked at the sign—the symbol of our desperation—we began to wonder what the many sick patients we had visited might have thought and felt when we arrived at their bedsides. Generally speaking, objectionable visitors fall into at least six distinct categories.

First is the hale and hearty type. He bursts into your hospital room like a cyclone—beaming and booming a lusty greeting. He often appears right after you have been wheeled from the recovery room, or the day after surgery. You look terrible. You feel terrible. You blink dazedly out of the stupor and smile through the nausea. You try to avoid a back-slapping, stitch-popping bear hug.

Who can forget the visitor with squatter's rights. She comes early and stays late. The victim may feign sleep, coughing attacks, sinking spells, or highly contagious disease, but nothing frightens or speeds the Squatter on her way. You are reduced to the role of a helpless, indignant spectacle. She takes in your every pain, every symptom, every treatment. Nothing escapes her observation.

Then the Indulger appears. He will present a huge and tempting box of candy or other smuggled goodies. It has been days since such gastronomic delicacies have come within sight or smelling distance. Faced with the temptation, you are tortured by the recollection of your doctor dictating a low-calorie, sugar-free, salt-free, fat-free, almost food-free diet. This visitor is akin to the one who brings bouquets of flowers or other pollen-loaded hazards to the asthma patient.

No illness is complete without the Prophet of Doom. She hovers at your bedside and solemnly shakes her head: "Yes, your symptoms are like those of my great-aunt, who lingered on for a little while before her horrible end." As your visitor recites this melancholy dirge, your mind begins to respond to her suggestions. *Yes,* you think, *I do have the same kind of pain! She is so sure.* Under your visitor's lamentations you break out with alternating cold sweats and burning fevers. Your imagination is activated by her graphic story from slight headache to brain tumor; from upset stomach to ptomaine poisoning; from faint rash to smallpox. When she finally leaves, you feel almost ready for the last rites.

Perhaps the most indiscreet visitor is the one who pries for details. No area of the patient's medical history or anatomy is sacred or secret as the most personal and embarrassing questions are asked. While some patients are eager to talk about their operations, many others are reluctant to share an intimate, stitch-by-stitch account with all the known world.

Finally, the sick visit the sick. I will never forget the student nurse who came to visit us the very day we brought our firstborn child home from the hospital. Being sensitive new parents, we had the apartment as sterile as humanly possible. Even so, our visitor insisted on holding our awesome and precious infant. Imagine our dismay when our visitor sighed: "What a relief to sit down. I have been on my feet all day in the tuberculosis ward!"

A similar feeling of despair and helplessness overwhelms the hospital patient as he receives the visitor who comes a-blowing, a-dripping, and a-coughing up to his bedside with a handshake, a hug, or perhaps a kiss. *The kiss of death!* thinks the patient.

The near relative to this type is the hospital visitor who fails to notice or take seriously the prominent sign that warns: NO SMOKING! OXYGEN EQUIPMENT IN USE!" He either wants to live dangerously or die violently. As he lights up, the captive patient begins a mental countdown from her bed. Blast-off will come any second.

Visiting the sick and infirm is a historic tradition and filled with moral implications, for none may depreciate the biblical injunction to "visit the sick" (Matt. 25:36). On the other hand, the patients are legion who have inwardly groaned: *I was sicker after you visited me."* Note this relevant council from a nationally recognized authority on health and healing:

"It is a misdirected kindness, a false idea of courtesy, that leads to much visiting of the sick. Those who are very ill should not have visitors. The excitement connected with receiving callers wearies the patient at a time when he is in the greatest need of quiet, undisturbed rest. To a convalescent or a patient suffering from chronic disease, it is often a pleasure and a benefit to know that he is kindly remembered; but this assurance conveyed by a message of sympathy or by some little gift will often serve a better purpose than a personal visit, and without danger of harm" (White 1905).

While visitation to the bedside of those that are seriously ill is always a worthy Christian mission, could we perform a greater service by a candid self-evaluation of our bedside manners and by revising our approach to the sickroom? As we minister in this way, we should disturb as little as possible the privacy, dignity, and peace of the patient. For is not a broken spirit as serious as a broken bone? Is not the healing of the body hindered or enhanced by the morale of the patient? (Bynum 2006)

# CHAPTER FOURTEEN

## The Keys to the Kingdom

My father was a great man. He loved his wife and children without reservation and served as our family foundation and leader until his untimely death in 1974. (I still miss you, Dad!) My father taught me to operate a farm tractor when I was twelve and to drive an old Model-A Ford when I was a sixteen-year-old teenager. When I was eighteen years old, I begged to use his nearly new Chevrolet sedan to take my first date to a high school program. Dad recognized how important that date was to me and loaned me his automobile for the occasion. Unfortunately, during the course of the evening, while I was gazing into the eyes of the girl, I managed to back Dad's car into a large tree, inflicting a small dent on the trunk. I felt terrible about the accident.

When I got home, I parked the Chevy in the garage, and with teenage logic, I rationalized that a night of rest would somehow heal the wounded trunk of my father's car. My heart sank the next morning when, from my bedroom window, I saw Dad open the garage door and drive his car out onto the driveway. He walked around until he paused to inspect the damage to the back of his new automobile. By the dawn's early light the small dent loomed as big as a bathtub. Then he got into his car and left for work. Several days passed while I tried to figure out how my meager resources might pay for the repair of Dad's car.

During that time, my father never said one word about the damaged car or digressed from his usual pleasant personality. Finally, I sorrowfully approached my father, told him how I had damaged his car, and promised to pay for the repairs—over time. Dad just smiled as he put his arm on my shoulder and refused my offer. I was close to tears when he said, "I understand how such things can happen. I am just glad that you were not hurt." Dad never did repair that dent in his Chevy. I regretted his eventual sale of that car because the ding in the trunk always reminded me of my father's dependable and unchanging love for me.

When I was twenty years old and had my own pride-and-joy first automobile—a 1950 Ford Club Coupe—my father offered me a much-needed bit of sage advice: "You can take off in that car without spinning the wheels." I patronizingly replied, "You can?" To which Dad answered, "You will learn that lesson after you pay for one or two sets of new tires." And sure enough—I did learn that lesson after exchanging my prematurely worn out original tires for new and expensive replacements. (I am a quick learner and replaced just *one* set of tires before that important lesson was learned). "It's what you learn after you know it all that counts" (John Wooden).

## Chariots and Horses

According to Shakespeare, in 1485 the forces of King Richard III of England were locked in combat against revolutionaries in the Battle of Bosworth Field. Richard and his bodyguard were cut off when his outnumbered soldiers attempted a strategic retreat. As his adversaries closed in, the desperate British monarch famously cried out: "A horse! A horse! My kingdom for a horse!" But no horse was available, and King Richard could not escape his death at the hand of the Earl of Richmond (Shakespeare 1592).

The importance of the horse as the practical and popular means of rapid transportation has been replaced in the last hundred years by the internal combustion engine mounted in wheeled vehicles. When the first motorized buggies sputtered down our roads, skeptical onlookers often shouted in derision: "Get a horse!" But the horseless carriages were here to stay.

Curiously, the variable power of gasoline engines is measured in horsepower. Thus, the V-8 engine of my first car was rated at 100 horsepower. And the horsepower race was on between competing automobile manufacturers who cultivated the belief that macho car purchasers demanded ever-increasing size and horsepower. Over the years, many modern automobile engines generating over 400 horsepower were developed. During the most recent decade, the inflating cost of fuel began to reverse and replace the horsepower race with a trend toward smaller, more fuel-efficient engines (Miller, et al. 2009).

Our American culture has continued to socialize members of society (especially males) into an intense love affair with wheeled transportation. Typically, it begins for many a young boy with a Radio Flyer Wagon—later nostalgically stored away in an attic or basement—as he graduates to tricycle, bicycle, and a Hot Wheels toy collection.

Then comes the proud and fulfilling day when the youth attains the keys to his first grown-up automobile. He thinks that the car keys (like a Harley-Davidson motorcycle tattoo) symbolize that he has successfully stormed the ramparts blocking his sacred destiny of manhood. Unlike the medieval king who was willing to bargain away his kingdom for a horse, our young man—astride the whirlwind of horsepower—has roared into the future. He expects to ride his mechanized metal steed into the kingdom of independent manhood.

Many times when I see and hear a youth screeching down the street in a car, hot rod, or pickup—with custom split manifold, twin exhaust pipes, and a blaring radio—I recognize the proud and public announcement that he has reached puberty and is someone to be reckoned with. In his mind, the car—with its big tires, big horsepower, big engine, and big noise—is the vehicle that symbolically transports him to a larger world. He assumes that the car will make him virile and important, lead to a paying job, and make him respected by males and attractive to females. "Here I am!" he is saying. "Look at me! Listen to me! I am somebody!" And throughout his life—even after the years mature his style and choice of vehicles—the car keys will remind him of the open road to freedom and the future—the coveted keys to the kingdom!

I will always remember my father's homespun wisdom. On my twenty-first birthday, when I was acting out the occasional foolish ideas and words of impetuous youth, Dad calmed me down by advising: "Although you are trying to prove that you are a man, you really won't be a man until you are about forty years old." Those were hard words for an ambitious and headstrong youth to swallow. But as I look back, it has become clear that my father's timetable was more accurate than mine— that true manhood is a maturity mellowed by time and experience. And I finally got my priorities straightened out: "Some trust in and boast of chariots, and some of horses, but we trust in and boast in the name of the Lord our God" (Ps. 20:7. AB).

## Driving by Committee

As we get older our proficiency and status as automobile drivers are subject to social review and change. My cousin Cleo laments that after forty-five years of driving the family car, he has been demoted. His unpardonable sins were running over the family cat in the driveway and getting disoriented in the Wal-Mart parking lot. His wife Mable and her mother (who now lives with them) never learned to drive, and their last child at home—a surly teenager named J.D.—was too young to get a driver's license. (Cleo confides that those initials stand for "Juvenile Delinquent").

As a result of these circumstances, driving by committee has evolved in their household. Cleo still gets to sit behind the steering wheel. Mabel rides shotgun, carries a large map, and issues obscure directions without using the words *left* or *right*. J.D. smirks in the back seat, itching to get his hands on the car keys. He functions as safety officer and watches for pedestrians, bicyclists, stop signs, and police cars. Cleo's mother-in-law also sits in the back seat and is in charge of hysterical screaming. Cleo describes their car on a family outing as "as a horrific concentration of human conflict and chaos in a small place."

## My Father's Car Keys

I finally grew up and Dad grew older. Our family and close friends noticed a slight decline in Dad's hearing and eyesight acuity and in his physical reflexes. We were getting worried about his possible decrease in driving skills. I was commissioned to ground him by asking for the ignition keys to his worn-out Ford pickup. While that approach had worked earlier for the children of a frail and elderly uncle, the Car Keys Surrender Proposal turned out to be easier said than done with my father! Dad was apparently oblivious to his growing reputation as an accident about to happen and continued to get into his pickup truck and make his daily rounds of post office, gasoline service station, shopping and church with Mom, and informal meetings in the park with his domino-playing buddies.

One day I found an excuse to go for a ride with my father. I must admit—other than a close shave between a bus and other vehicles, and a shortcut down the sidewalk—Dad did surprisingly well. When I jokingly commented that "such a ride could change my prayer life," Dad replied, "I'll not be surrendering my keys or giving up my truck!" And he never did! "Regarding your prayer life," he continued, "Men ought always to pray, and not to faint" (Luke 18:1).

## History Repeats Itself

I also have a son. We have a warm and close relationship. In many ways, he is like me—a chip off the old block. When he was a college student, he drove my best car on a flower-gathering expedition. There was a minor accident in which the car slipped off the shoulder of the road, burst through a barbed wire fence, and plowed to a stop in a cow pasture. Though scraped and roughed up a bit, the car was still drivable, and was waiting for me when I arrived home.

My son—together with his mother, sister, and brother-in-law— were anxiously awaiting my arrival and watched me silently inspect the damaged automobile. I estimated that repairs could cost seven hundred dollars or more. I was also remembering my own father's reaction when I brought home his damaged car after my youthful evening of careless driving. So turning to my worried family, forlornly huddled in the yard, I bit my lip and said: "I am so thankful that no one was hurt in this accident. Don't worry. I have had some experience in such matters and will take this car to a repair shop tomorrow. Now—what's for dinner?"

The years have passed, and my son is now a distinguished physician with children of his own. Paradoxically, I notice that my family is starting to ask subtle questions about my driving habits. To my credit, the State Department of Motor Vehicles recently renewed my driver's license for another eight years!

Nevertheless—I was disturbed a little by the clumsy examination for visual and mental comprehension at the DMV. The clerk held up her hand and asked, "What do you see?" I assume that the clerk wanted to find out if I could still recognize a human hand, and if I could still accurately count up to five fingers. I passed the test with flying colors. Last week, my son went for a pleasant ride with me around town. Medical school must have been an inspiration to him because he likes to make "doctor-talk" about things like pulse rates, blood pressure, respiration, and reflex/reactions. He also has a curious interest in my car keys. Sometimes I wonder what he is thinking.

# CHAPTER FIFTEEN

## A Pioneer Family

M any retirees become avid students of genealogy—the study of family history and descent. For example, My wife and I have found an ongoing survey of our family roots both fascinating and rewarding. This elderly interest may be an unconscious impulse to clarify the overarching context and meanings of our own lives. As I mentioned earlier, Margaret descended from pioneer settlers that migrated on the Oregon Trail into the Pacific Northwest. A few more genealogical details are appropriate here. Her great-grandfather William Powell and his family entered the Oregon Territory shortly after the American Civil War. Powell's strong support for the Union cause was reflected in the naming of his first son: Thaddeus Lincoln Powell—who was destined to become Margaret's maternal grandfather.

William Powell and his family helped develop the small Southern Oregon town of Ashland in the 1880s when the community consisted of little more than a train depot for the Southern Pacific Railroad and small flour and woolen mills located on Ashland Creek. The Powell men were industrious builders and businessmen and eventually owned several homes and considerable acreage in and around Ashland. Like the legendary Johnny Appleseed, they planted numerous apple orchards and operated a rudimentary press to produce apple cider. William was nicknamed The Apple Cider Man when he began selling refreshing apple cider from a picturesque wooden cart to train passengers stopping at the new SP depot. The famous pioneer man statue on the central plaza in downtown Ashland commemorates early settlers like William Powell.

Southern Oregon became well-known for a variety of local beverages: a natural spring of bitter, high-powered, mineral water called Lithia water, Powell's apple cider, and Ornico, an organic mineral concentrate used by some residents as a folk remedy for numerous ailments and injuries.

Thaddeus Powell was still alive when I met his granddaughter Margaret at a Northern California college in 1953. She was a beautiful and refined Christian girl, a good student, and with extraordinary musical and artistic talents. When I traveled up to Ashland to meet Margaret's family, the thought crossed my mind that a wife from such hardy pioneer stock could bring resourceful strength and stamina to our marriage. I fantasized that we would never go hungry because my wife's pioneer heritage would send her forth with a shotgun or bow and arrow to shoot an elk or buffalo for our table. She would not be spoiled by modern, expensive furniture or equipment. For example, rather than having to purchase an automatic clothes washer, she could probably wash our clothes Indian fashion—on a good rock down by the creek. These thoughts turned out to be just the whimsical fantasies of my youth. Margaret was indeed industrious and hard-working, but she also had reasonable matrimonial expectations about the marriage, family, and home we would establish.

Our genealogical research also revealed that I am the product of another old American family dating back to the eighteenth-century colonies. After the American Civil War, a large number of Bynum family pioneers followed the advancing American frontier from the old Confederate South through Texas and into California. The two old pioneer families were joined when Margaret and I were married in 1954. My following career led us to live for periods of time in California, Oregon, Idaho, Washington, Oklahoma and Texas.

When I retired from my teaching profession in 2000, Margaret and I returned to live in her hometown of Ashland, Oregon. While I maintained part-time academic involvement with Southern Oregon State University,

Margaret's interest in her local family roots was intensified. Last year, she was delighted to hear that the Ashland Historical Society Museum was sponsoring a summer series of dramatizations in the old pioneer cemetery. Costumed actors—wearing authentic period clothing of the 1880s—would move among the ornate, old-fashioned gravestones and act out the roles of eight Ashland pioneers. One of those early settlers to be impersonated was William Powell, the Ashland Cider Man! I escorted a highly-pleased Margaret and her sister Marianne as they followed the actors and heard the colorful stories of Ashland pioneers—especially that of their great-grandfather, William Powell.

## We Love a Parade!

Margaret is one of six sisters, and their husbands and progeny—plus other prolific branches of a large extended family—have spread throughout the Northwestern states. And many of them are still clustered in or near Ashland, Oregon. A few relatives have participated in the unique Kiltie Band—a group of bag pipers, attired in the traditional kilts and tartans of old Scotland—that march in the annual Independence Day Parade.

Other members of Margaret's family have also surprisingly participated in local parades. For instance, a few years ago, Audie—a brother-in-law married to Margaret's sister, Betty—spontaneously flung himself off the curb directly into the path of a very large and unusual vehicle that was bouncing along the parade route on huge rubber tires. The crowd gasped as people believed they were about to witness a frightening disaster. But Audie knew better. After the big balloon tires rolled harmlessly over his body, he laughingly jumped to his feet and rejoined us on the curb. There was relieved applause as the people realized that they were recipients of unexpected entertainment and a colossal practical joke.

On another occasion, my wife and I were spectators at a long parade in Moscow, Idaho, and we had gotten temporarily separately in the crowd near the end of the parade. The final segment included a group of seven- and eight-year-old kids driving a dozen homemade, battery-powered go-carts. When one go-cart stalled, the two small children inside became confused and distressed as the other children and go-carts passed them on the way to the finish line.

I was astonished to see a small grandmother–type woman resolutely rush from the sidelines into the street and laboriously push the stalled go-cart and its' passengers two blocks to the finish line. It was my wife, Margaret! Later, when I pointed out to her that our grandchildren were not in the parade—and asked her *why* she performed that exhausting and heroic action—Margaret simply answered: "I don't know—except those two little kids looked so helpless and sad." But I know why she did it. My wife has a big heart. And she listens to her heart, especially when children are involved.

The parade judges awarding prizes to the various entries felt obliged to rank Margaret with the group of animals because of the nature of her performance. Unfortunately, she lost out in the Blue Ribbon competition in that group to a team of big Clydesdale horses pulling the Budweiser Beer Wagon.

# CHAPTER SIXTEEN

## What Time is it? *"Tempus Fugit"*

From the very beginning of human history, the daily and seasonal fluctuations in light, darkness, weather, and the availability of shelter and food have intrigued mankind. Our earliest ancestors observed that changes in these natural phenomena occur in predictable patterns associated with the passage of time. In addition, temporal events on earth reflect a mysterious connection with the sun. Many primitive tribes—in crediting the growth and harvest of their food plants to the presence of a warm and dominant sun—began to worship the sun as their god. They assumed that the sun was the fundamental force, source, and sustainer of life. By imputing deity to a heavenly body that could be seen and experienced, many people looked no further for an invisible, abstract, and original creator God.

To counter this misconception of the sun as the primary and divine cause in the universe may have motivated Moses to write the Old Testament story of an all-powerful and infinite God who created everything and who set the sun, earth, and life in motion over time and space. In the New Testament of the Bible, God discloses His divine purpose and plan behind the wonders of creation (John 1).

In the first chapter of the Bible, Moses describes the beginning of human experience and history. It is a profound and primary description of God's command and control of time in the creation of the earth and mankind. The weekly cycle of seven twenty-four-hour days is used as a framework to explain God's creative work to a people with limited knowledge of systematic theology, astronomy, and the natural world. Centuries later, scientists would support and detail the Genesis account of a daily rotation of the earth on its axis with alternating periods of darkness and light as our planet reacts to the presence of an impersonal sun.

Early scientists also unraveled the mystery of the annual cycle of a 365-day orbit of the earth around the sun—accounting for the seasonal changes of winter, spring, summer, and fall. With growing knowledge regarding the dimensions of chronological time (hours, days, months, and years), time became an increasingly valuable commodity and factor in the lives of human beings. Older people more than young people—having experienced the lifelong demands of clocks, calendars, schedules and deadlines—are probably more aware of valuable and irretrievable time.

## The Clock Man

A few years ago I chanced to meet an unusual character known as The Oregon Clock Man (also known in Southern Oregon as Father Time). This elderly and eccentric gentleman proudly and publically announced his nickname by wearing an assortment of twelve or more watches on his wrists and forearms. When I observed him I could not resist the temptation to ask: "What time is it?" And Father Time responded: "These old watches no longer keep accurate time. They are works of art, and I wear them as symbolic accessories. If you will visit my house I will give you the exact time for all time zones in the world, explain the International Date Line and Daylight Saving Time, and show you my entire clock and watch collection."

As we walked the two blocks to the Clock Man's cottage, I became aware of an odd and annoying little sound—synchronized with every step he took. It was an audible clicking sound coming from his mouth: "Tick—tock. Tick—tock. Tick—tock." Apparently, the clock man had taken on a major characteristic of a clock—and he may have been wound too tight!

His front yard contained a large sundial and a small model of Stonehenge—massive stone ruins in England erected between 3000 and 1500 BC. Speculations as to the original purpose of the site suggest that Stonehenge may have been an ancient pagan religious temple. Some nineteenth-century scholars pointed to the orientation of the monument entrance to the rising sun on the day of the summer solstice. This suggests that ancient tribes in the area may have used Stonehenge as a kind of solar calendar to track the movement of the sun and moon and mark the changing seasons (Rosamund, Walker, and Montague 1995).

The interior of Father Time's small house contained a startling display of thousands of broken and worn-out clocks and watches—totally covering every wall, from baseboard to ceiling. More time pieces dangled from the ceilings. The man's hobby of collecting clocks and watches had become a fetish—an obsessive, uncontrollable hoard of dysfunctional time pieces. I saw no expensive, gold-plated Rolex watches—or even an old-fashioned children's Orphan Annie watch in the collection. Generally, they were cheap, made-in-China, throwaway watches. But Father Time was a virtual walking and talking encyclopedia on time and time pieces. He had answers to questions no one ever asks. He was pleased and proud of his collection and was clearly disappointed when I finally excused myself and left. The last I heard was that The Clock Man had passed away. It was an untimely death.

## My Great-Grandmother's Clock

To a lesser but significant degree, most of us are controlled by the constraints and boundaries of time. We are constantly monitored and reminded of passing time by parking meters, microwave ovens, auto speedometers, musical metronomes, rocket launch countdowns, taxicab meters, and hundreds of other devices. Our servitude to time began in childhood when we were taught how to write our names, tie our shoelaces, and how to tell time. Attentive respect for passing time is deeply ingrained in our culture that extols punctuality and constructive work—and a large measure of guilt for wasting time. Personally, I was first introduced to time just four days after I was born.

When my parents took me home from the hospital, I met my mother's widowed and aged grandmother who lived with us. As it turned out, my first year of life was her last year of life. As my great-grandmother was gently rocking me to sleep, she remarked to my mother, "This is my first great-grandchild. What can I give to him?" At that very moment, her exquisite antique clock on the fireplace mantel chimed the hour. And Great-Grandmother exclaimed, "This little boy shall have that old clock as my heirloom to him." And so it was. Though the clock is now over 150 years old, it still keeps perfect time and has an honored place on an old-fashioned pump organ in our Ashland home. And every time that old clock chimes the beginning of a new hour, it reminds us again of a great-grandmother's love for a newborn baby.

## My Father's Clock

My father was a building contractor who designed and constructed many fine homes. He was also a skilled craftsman who built several beautiful pieces of early American furniture as a hobby. During his middle years, Dad was inspired to extend and reinforce our family traditions with a handmade grandfather clock. He ordered an Emperor grandfather clock mechanism—together with the face, chimes, pendulum, and weights—from the manufacturer. Then he set about assembling a long-case cabinet of cherry wood to house the clock. After applying a rich walnut stain and adjusting the clock mechanism, Dad gathered the family to present his gift to future generations.

His grandfather clock was over six feet, three inches tall and stood in the family home in California until both of my parents passed away. Fearing that I might damage the fragile clock in transporting it all the way to our home in Oregon, I gave my father's grandfather clock to our daughter and her family who lived just a hundred miles away. They respect the clock as a symbol of our intergenerational love and durability and take good care of it.

## My Grandfather Clock

I could surrender Dad's clock early to the next generation because shortly before he died, he ordered two more of the same clock mechanisms and challenged my brother and me to build, assemble, and finish the cabinets for two more grandfather clocks in the family. It proved to be a difficult assignment for me. Other than elementary hammer and saw carpentry experience, I lacked the necessary skills to build a grandfather clock. Fortunately, I was well aware of my shortcomings and took a very slow and methodical approach to the project—with each small step preceded by lengthy research and consultations with furniture and cabinet builders. Special problems were the production and fitting of mitered corners, installation of the intricate clock mechanism, and the hanging of fragile, glass-paned access doors.

I was haunted by two Latin words inscribed across the face of the clock urging me to pursue the clock project with vigor: *"Tempus Fugit"* or "Time Flies!" The face seemed to shout at me to get busy and complete the task. It took several months of my spare time before the finishing touches gave my grandfather clock a stately presence in our living room. I mounted my small brass nameplate and the date near the face of the clock. A small hook on the back attached the top-heavy clock to the wall, thus securing it against the possibility of falling on small children in the family.

I am an elderly man now, and my grandfather clock will eventually go to my son, who in turn will pass the family heirloom on to one of his children to cherish and care for before passing it on to the next generation. (The same process of transfer will take place as my father's grandfather clock is passed through our daughter's descendants.) Thus, the branches and members of our family will be connected as they see and hear the faithful old grandfather clocks moving and ticking their way through our generations—measuring out the spans of our lives. This reminds me of a wonderful old folk song:

> My grandfather's clock was too large for the shelf,
> So it stood ninety years on the floor,
> It was taller by half than the old man himself,
> Though it weighed not a pennyweight more,
> It was bought on the morn of the day that he was born,
> And was always his treasure and pride;

> But it stopp'd short—never to go again-
> When the old man died.
> CHORUS:
> Ninety years without slumbering
> (tick, tock, tick, tock),
> His life's seconds numbering,
> (tick, tock, tick, tock),
> And it stopp'd short—never to go again-
> When the old man died.
>
> (Henry Clay Work 1876)

～

## "Come Apart and Rest Awhile" (Mark 6:31)

Contrary to reputation, time is not just an irresistible taskmaster offering structure, organization, and direction for our lives and labor. True, in my younger years I was very much a young man in a hurry. The principle of *tempus fugit* was applied to every facet of life—in my impatient and eager pursuit of education, career, and other objectives. I never paused long in the valleys of defeat or indecision, or on the mountain tops of achievement, but bowing to the tyranny of time, I rushed on to the challenges of still higher mountains on the horizon.

Finally, I realized that passing time—recorded by our clocks and calendars—is not just the vehicle to remind us of our calling to duty or work, no matter how noble. Nor is our knowledge and sense of passing time solely a reminder of birthdays, holidays, anniversaries, New Years, and other upcoming events and celebrations—no matter how significant. Nor is the chronological marking of time intended just to facilitate intergenerational cohesion and heritage, as symbolized by the grandfather clocks in my family. While these obvious and practical purposes are extremely important and beneficial, my discovery of the larger blessing of time was still ahead of me.

When I approached manhood, I learned from experience that even young and strong men can eventually fall with exhaustion under the incessant demands of work. It was then that I learned a new and important lesson about time. In the beginning, the creator God balanced each day with portions of light and darkness—light favorable to work and darkness conducive to rest—followed by the awakening dawn of another day and again the setting sun of nightfall (Gen. 1).

In other words, the passing of time in the natural world illustrates the intrinsic relationship between active labor and reflective rest. Thus, there are two complimentary dimensions of our time: day and night; light and darkness, work and rest. Logically, how and from what can we rest unless our rest is preceded by labor? Conversely, how can we do our best work unless preceded by restorative rest? Later, in the Ten Commandments, God recognized this balanced equilibrium in commemorated His creation by crowning the seven-day weekly cycle with a day of rest for humanity (Ex. 20).

## The Tonic of Time

Over and above that original formula for physical well-being, the same God who instructed us to alternately work and rest is also continually attentive to our need for spiritual rejuvenation. "Come unto me" Jesus said. "Come unto me, all ye that are heavy laden, and I will give you rest" (Matt. 11:28). He takes no pleasure in seeing us discouraged and crushed by the weight of our guilt and mistakes, our unfinished labors and unfulfilled objectives.

Clearly, the clock and the calendar that call us to work also call us to rest. But when we periodically cease from our labors, we are more than physically rested. Spiritual peace, joy, hope, and vision can also be restored and renewed in us through the miracle of passing time. Innumerable multitudes of people have found healing for body, mind, and soul through the tonic of time.

One of the most important discoveries of my life has been that hard work, struggle, and sweat cannot resolve or fix everything. Yes, there are some things that come quickly to us, but there are other things, important things, that take time. So it is futile to try to force every issue, to force happiness, to force hurt hearts to heal. There is much that we must leave to the slow and silent power of time. Much that we fret about at the moment doesn't seem so much when we wait awhile.

Passing time heals old hurts. It dulls the edge of deep disappointment. It clears up many misunderstandings. It makes old feuds fade. Time tempers the rashness of youth and ripens wisdom. It favors truth and exposes falsehood. Time cools hot tempers. It mellows men. The long view afforded by passing time can sharpen our perspective and reorder our priorities.

> "And as for sorrows: some of them can only be quieted by the softening touch of time—not by a quick touch, but with much moving of the clock and much changing of the calendar—maybe days, maybe months, maybe years—but the Tonic of Time is a proven and reliable cure. Though it seems at first that the sharp hurt to the soul will never be softened, we shall have to wait for time to pass.

> "Yes, there are some things we can force; some things we can rush—but not the subsiding of sorrow; not love; not full understanding; not personal peace. These are things we must leave to the softening touch— the tonic of time" (Source unknown).

# CHAPTER SEVENTEEN

## The Hometown Hero

Margaret and I have a favorite fast-food café in Ashland—sandwiched among a dozen other small stores and shops around the downtown plaza. Appropriately, the patrons of the Hometown Hero are a comfortable mix of tourists, hikers from the Pacific Crest Trail, and locals who like the food and the laid-back atmosphere. The casual eatery is named after The Hero—the famous and featured centerpiece of the menu. In the opinion of many who have eaten it, this large and delightful sandwich is an unforgettable experience that features generous layers of quality cheeses or cold cuts, fresh lettuce, veggies, pickles, olives, and choices of seven or eight seasonings, sauces, and condiments—all overloaded on a long, split roll of Italian or French bread. In short, The Hero is the greatest sandwich Margaret and I have ever eaten, and we are regulars at the popular Hometown Hero restaurant.

Recently, while exploring and munching my way through a one-pound Hero, I became curious about the name of the restaurant and the sandwich. What was its origin? What is the meaning? Does the special sandwich require a gastronomic hero to consume it all? Or does the sandwich have the magic power to transform customers into heroes to defend the weak and battle villains in the community—like Popeye who gained superhuman strength from a diet of spinach.

One must be careful in the use of descriptive metaphors because accuracy of meaning can be lost in translation or communication to others. For example, President John Kennedy eloquently declared his oneness with the hard-pressed citizens of Berlin, Germany, during the Cold War by dramatically announcing: *"Ich bin ein Berliner!"* ("I am a Berliner!"). Kennedy was unaware that a Berliner is also the name of a popular German pastry. Some commentators still insist that one embarrassing translation of Kennedy's declaration is: "I am a jelly donut!" So I must be careful not to impute more or less to the Hero sandwich than it deserves.

My curiosity led me to inquire of the manager of the Hometown Hero restaurant regarding the source of the unique name of the special sandwich. She briefly replied that the popular sandwich originated among Italian-Americans living in the northeastern states between the late nineteenth and mid-twentieth centuries. Regional origins and variations are reflected in the different names of submarine, hoagie, hero, and grinder for the sandwich.

## The Hero Sandwich War

In pursuit of more specific information, my investigation turned up some fascinating details regarding the origin and source of the Hero name attached to the sandwich. In 1890, Richmond Turnpike in New York City was renamed Victory Boulevard, coinciding with the creation of Hero Park to commemorate the site of the original hero sandwich designed by Armando Vespucci. It was also the spot where Staten Island volunteers won an astonishing victory over the New Jersey militia in a conflict known as The Hero Sandwich War (or The Food Patent Riots).

The trouble started when Vespucci, owner of a roadhouse and inn located on the current site of Hero Park, decided to patent the most popular item on his menu, a large sandwich filled with almost every item in the kitchen on a slab of Italian bread. Vespucci called the dish "a sandwich of heroic proportions." It became something of a sensation in nineteenth-century Staten Island, and locals referred to it simply as The Hero.

Word quickly spread to nearby Bayonne, New Jersey, where Angus MacMurtry had added the same item to the offerings in his restaurant.

Faced with the prospect of Vespucci's pending patent restricting use of the sandwich and suspicious of foul play by Vespucci, MacMurtry rallied some members of the New Jersey militia and embarked by ferry to Staten Island, New York, to arrest Vespucci.

When the militia marched down the Richmond Turnpike (the current Victory Boulevard), word of the New Jersey invasion spread through the neighborhood. Local citizens flocked to the defense of Vespucci and his culinary creation. Out-gunned (some Staten Islanders had nothing but dried salamis, which they used as clubs), but superior in numbers, they were able to drive back the New Jersey invaders after a horrific battle.

The question about the rights to the hero sandwich patent would go through a long series of litigation and was finally decided by the U.S. Supreme Court. In a split decision, authored by Chief Justice Roger Taney, the court ruled that no one could patent a sandwich, thus rendering ownership moot (Artist Recreation 2011).

## A Culture of Hero Worship

Although my curiosity was satisfied about the origin of the name for my favorite sandwich, I became convinced that I had just explored the tip of the hero concept. A real hero is much more than a sandwich. Yet to be examined was the massive history and explanation of our human preoccupation with heroes.

Numerous observers of the phenomena have concluded that the definition of a hero cannot be separated from the life, purpose, and behavior of the individual so identified. Thus, by definition, a hero (or the feminine equivalent of heroine) is a person of myth or reality who has demonstrated distinguished courage and ability in the service of society. The hero is so designated by others and regarded as a model or ideal for his or her brave deeds and noble qualities (*Webster's World English Dictionary* 1998).

We typically enter and participate in a widespread culture of hero-worship as young children admiring many heroic individuals—both real and fictitious. My parents were early enshrined in my childhood Hall of Heroes. And they instilled in me a lifelong religious reverence for the Lord—later described in a rock opera *as Jesus Christ Superstar* (Rice and Weber 1971). I also sat in awe at the feet of returning World War II soldiers and marveled at their stories and battle scars. I vicariously participated through books in the exploits of brave explorers of history. A more fantasized category of heroes also lived in my boyish imagination. In my daydreams, I rode with the Lone Ranger and Tonto in bringing justice to the western frontier.

When I was ten years old, hero worship once prompted me to don the cape and costume of Superman and perilously launch myself off the garage roof. We neighborhood youngsters fought many a battle with wooden swords and wearing cardboard armor as knights of King Arthur's Round Table. I was especially entranced with Sir Lancelot, who had humbly declared: "My strength is as the strength of ten because my heart is pure." My leap of faith and painful landing off the garage roof demonstrated the limitations of my strength. Meanwhile—back at Camelot—Guinevere proved that there were definite limitations to Lancelot's purity.

As an adult, most of my heroes are wise and resourceful leaders like George Washington and Abraham Lincoln who saved and shaped our country. Similarly, I greatly admire the brilliant scholars and scientists whose intellectual contributions have greatly improved human civilization or conquered many dread diseases. My current heroes also include military warriors who often suffer incredible hardships to protect our country, astronauts who are pioneering space exploration, dedicated surgeons who battle death in the operating rooms, and several outstanding athletes.

Finally, although I have accumulated many years, there is still room in my heart for the imaginary and idealistic hero of childhood. However, like many other old-timers, I see the youthful strength and agility of body and mind now transforming into the fumbling, fragile, and forgetful caricature of old age. The heroic and handsome heroes of my childhood have also grown old.

For instance, Don Quixote—the man of La Mancha—often comes galloping of the pages of Cervantes' classic novel and across the horizon of my elderly imagination. The ancient Spanish knight is the personification of manly chivalry—ever searching for dragons to slay, fair maidens to rescue, and noble causes for which to risk life and limb. But admittedly, the man of La Mancha is an aged, demented, incompetent knight with an impossible dream and obsessive quest for truth, justice, and love. In a world that is ugly, cruel, and selfish, Quixote sees beauty and nobility in everything because that is what he wishes to see. So he spends his life righting wrongs, idealizing love, and forgiving his enemies. There are nearly four hundred years between Don Quixote and me, but he will always live—idealized in the impossible dreams of old men like me who are still looking for heroes to emulate and follow (Cervantes 2000). In the meantime, I'm heading downtown for another Hero sandwich!

## The Unsung Heroes

Contrary to the highly publicized and celebrated heroes of the battlefield, athletic field, laboratory, literature, and political arena, the majority of heroes and heroines avoid the limelight and perform their noble deeds of sacrifice and service in the background. However, without their silent and supporting sidekicks, most of our renowned heroes would probably never have reached center stage. For example, Don Quixote would have probably been insignificant without Sancho, his unglamorous page. And the Lone Ranger—with his celebrated mask, white horse, and triumphant shout "Hi ho, Silver! Away!"—was clearly a cinema hero. But Tonto, the Lone Ranger's faithful Indian companion—while also fighting for truth and justice—was almost invisible. Their dialogue is seldom more than this example: The Lone Ranger: "Tonto, you wait here with the horses while I go into town." Tonto: *"Kemo sabi."* (It is sadly and ironically purported that the name Tonto means "stupid" or "fool" in Spanish. And "kemo sabi" in one American Indian dialect translates: "He who knows nothing.")

Margaret and I have our eyes open for the unsung heroes in our lives and hometown. These are the humble people who, through their generally unnoticed day-by-day heroics, serve the greater good of society. They remind us of the higher and nobler purpose of our lives. I covet the association and friendship of such quiet and unselfish heroes.

One such hero that attracted our attention is fifteen-year-old Eric Sumner, who observed two older and larger boys cruelly taunting and touching a crying girl in the hall of their high school. Without hesitation, Eric intervened by stepped between the girl and the bullies. A growing crowd of other students gathered to watch the confrontation. Eric fought gallantly, but was finally knocked down. As Eric scrambled back to his feet, his best friend Mark arrived and together with two other girls came to his assistance. The example of one hero inspired honor and bravery in others as they vanquished the school bullies. Eric and his allies remind me of the creed of the ancient Spartan warriors who were often outnumbered on the battlefield: "Good shall overcome evil! We are the Spartans, and we shall prevail!"

Recently, another hero was reported in the newspapers. Max Kulenowski, an unemployed and homeless man, was peddling his bicycle through town late one night when he noticed smoke and flames coming from an old house. He paused in the street when a woman appeared at a second floor window and screamed for help. Max quickly awakened neighbors who telephoned for help.

While the fire department was on the way, Max returned to the woman in the window. The fire was spreading rapidly, and she was choking on the smoke. She told Max that she and her small child were alone and trapped upstairs. Max is a small and elderly man, but he braced himself and instructed the woman to toss the child out to him. Miraculously, Max successfully caught the four-year-old and handed him to nearby neighbors. Then he told the woman to jump. In desperation from the approaching fire, she leaped toward Max's outreaching arms. She also was unhurt, but Max was knocked down with multiple contusions and sprains. As arriving firemen swarmed into the yard, Max got on his bicycle and faded away into the darkness. It took two more days before grateful townspeople located Max—the modest hero.

There are potential heroes everywhere—all around us and perhaps even dormant in you and me. The true heroes are often unlikely individuals whom we would never cast in that role. We don't know in advance who they are, and they don't know either. It requires a special situation or opportunity to cause those with the right stuff to step forward and take action. Real heroes can be of any age, race, nationality, religion, or political persuasion. They spontaneously and personally respond to the immediate need for courage and compassion.

Many women—generally assigned to a more passive role in society—have emerged as unsung heroines in supporting their husbands and children achieve high goals and aspirations. Over and over, I have seen unassuming widows, wives, and mothers—with only meager strength and financial resources—valiantly raise tuition money so family members could attend college.

One middle-aged widow of our acquaintance was a clerk in a small grocery. When her daughter graduated from high school, there was not enough money for the girl to attend college. Without hesitation, that devoted and resourceful mother walked many miles along the roads on weekends and evenings after her regular work, picking up discarded aluminum cans. Over a period of four years, the small deposits on hundreds of thousands of discarded aluminum cans paid most of her daughter's college tuition. Many friends saved their cans and contributed them to the cause. That heroic mother saw her daughter graduate from college, marry her college sweetheart, and launch her own professional career.

I believe that a great many of us—when looking back over our lives and rummaging among the memories—could identify a supportive, self-effacing parent, sibling, friend, husband, or wife who believed in us and made tremendous sacrifices in our behalf. They are the unsung heroes or heroines standing in the shadows, and who made it possible for us to fulfill our hopes and dreams. The beautiful ballad "Wind Beneath My Wings" sublimely expresses our acknowledgement of the secret and silent heroes in our lives:

> It must have been cold there in my shadow
> To never have sunlight on your face
> You've been content to let me shine
> You always walked a step behind
>
> I was the one with all the glory
> While you were the one with all the strength

Only a face without a name
I never once heard you complain

Did you ever know that you're my hero
And everything I'd like to be
I can fly higher than an eagle
But you are the wind beneath my wings

It might have appeared to go unnoticed
But I've got it all here in my heart
I want you to know I know the truth
I would be nothing without you

Did you ever know that you're my hero
And everything I'd like to be
I can fly higher than an eagle
But you are the wind beneath my wings.

—Jeff Silbar and Larry Henley (1982)

# CHAPTER EIGHTEEN

## The Political Jungle

When I retired from my salaried occupation, I noticed an increased interest in politics among many elderly voters. Their growing partisan discussion and debate may be fueled by such issues as age-related health problems and the viability of Social Security. So we seniors actually listened during the last election year when Senator Bulartis* came to town—followed by numerous other candidates for Congress and the State Assembly.

The advance agents for the various politicians would have the residents believe that the long-anticipated Second Coming was eminent. Local cynics suspect that Ashland is only honored by the periodic presence of campaigning politicians because our town has a reputation for a pleasing variety of food and entertainment. Ashland is also on U.S. Interstate Highway 5—the main south/north ground transportation artery through Oregon.

Already present on the scene was a host of local county and city politicians with their posters, pictures, and pronouncements competing for attention and votes. Public meetings and campaign rallies are held where sparse crowds of tourists, street people, and retirees may pause to hear immodest claims from candidates of past accomplishments and promises of future glory for Ashland, the nation, and the world. Apparently, a social utopia is just round the corner!

When the senator's caravan and entourage arrived, he joined with local representatives of his party and civic leaders for a short and noisy inspection of the university campus, Lithia Park, and a construction site before settling down in a hotel conference room for a catered meal and carefully orchestrated news conference. When mingling with the common people in the streets, Senator Bulartis and his aides removed their coats and neckties, unbuttoned their collars, and partially rolled up the sleeves of their dress shirts to appear as "working" in the photo-op. At the construction site, the resourceful candidate may borrow a hard hat as news cameras zoom in so he will look like he just got off a bulldozer. [*Senator Bulartis is a composite characterization of many politicians].

## The Political Independent

Although the political roots of my family are deep, my personal involvement has been shallow. My father was a staunch supporter of his trade union and the Democratic Party. My mother was a faithful member of the WCTU and the Republican Party. They never discussed politics at home, but as far back as I can remember, when Election Day arrived they got into the family car together and merrily departed to cast their ballots—effectively cancelling out one another's vote. Little wonder then—that during my adulthood, I have waffled in my voter registrations between the Democratic and Republican parties. In recent years, I have tried to compromise my uncertain political affiliation by registering as an Independent.

There are some advantages to identifying myself as politically Independent. I can appear aloof from the fanatical election battles between many Democrats and Republicans who feel duty-bound to religiously promote and defend every iota of their respective party platforms. We Independents like to assume a posture of political neutrality—calmly weighing each issue with a nonpartisan objectivity before rendering our unbiased decisions. People who don't know me very well often misinterpret my uncertainty for political discernment. On the downside, the self-proclaimed political independent may be simultaneously courted and cursed by both liberal left and conservative right extremes of the political spectrum for withholding or delaying his or her full commitment and support.

## Political Irrelevance

Getting back to the election year campaign visits to our town, many locals have observed that very few of the candidates' public announcements, pronouncements, and denouncements offer any substantive solutions to pressing *local issues,* such as the growing numbers of unemployed vagrants bedding down in Lithia Park and on the plaza, or the declining availability of irrigation water and public transportation. Most of the political utterances of our visitors from out-of-town focus on broad and abstract issues like world peace, the national debt, global warming, and fossil fuels. While not denying the importance of these larger topics, when some listener tries to bring up our local and personal political concerns, time often runs out and the politicians hurry off to their next appointment.

I am reminded that I had seen this scenario before. A president of the United States was delivering his last presidential speech to a stadium full of university students, faculty, and alumni when some impoverished and struggling students tried in vain to get his attention to their personal economic dilemma. Two of them suddenly laid aside their clothing, and with campus police in hot pursuit, they streaked across the stage. The President retained his cool and never paused or missed a beat in his carefully structured political address on the world economy. At the end of his speech, he *did* attempt a humorless joke by hoping "that college student get their student loans paid off before applying for Social Security."

## Professors versus Politicians

My close contacts with politicians have been meager but revealing. For example, in 1981 one of my research studies suggested that carefully-screened, young men—imprisoned for nonviolent crimes—be allowed to voluntarily serve their prison time in our military forces. Such a program could simultaneously save money on their prison incarceration and add many healthy recruits to our armed forces. Even more important, honorable military service could give these young men a new opportunity to a positive and productive future in society. My model was the French Foreign Legion, an elite military force that includes many rehabilitated men with criminal backgrounds. The Legion received more citations for bravery and faithfulness to duty during World War II than any other combat brigade (Bynum and Downing 1981).

As this innovative idea was publicized through the news media, I was vigorously challenged by several State legislators who argued in a public radio debate that "our military recruits should always demonstrate the highest standards of character and former criminals could not be trusted in the armed forces." My academic colleagues and I countered that "many of our political leaders have served in public office despite evidence of past character flaws and even criminal conduct."

The politicians then contended that "young men fresh from a prison environment would be difficult to control and train for military service." To which I recalled many years ago how my capable Army First Sergeant—through precept and example—instilled "the fear of God and love of country" into new recruits of big farm boys, former gang members, and other tough guys who dared to test his authority. Under the leadership and guidance of Sgt. R.J. Horn, nearly all of those challenging and unpromising recruits became loyal and dependable soldiers.

Nothing came from the tempest of that political debate and the issue soon died. The professors may have had the strongest argument, but the politicians had the legislative power. However, a few months later I was surprised to receive a large and impressive certificate carrying the official seal of the Oklahoma House of Representatives in the state capital. It was an honorary citation for my "sociological teaching, research, and service to the people of Oklahoma." Such a magnanimous gesture demonstrated that mature politicians and professors can participate in a good fight and have honest differences of opinion without residual grudges. It reinforced my faith in the democratic process.

# CHAPTER NINETEEN

## Senior Citizens: Romance and Courtship

### The Ten-Foot Pole

Times have certainly changed! I read of a conservative college back in the 1930s where male and female students were forbidden to walk side by side on a path (Utt 1996, pp. 11–14, 23). For years, there was an unverified rumor among some students that the dormitory dean of women actually kept a symbolic, ten-foot-long pole in her office as a reminder of the rule forbidding unauthorized contact between the sexes. Perhaps that fable was the source of the old colloquialism: "I wouldn't touch that—(or it, or him, or her)—with a ten-foot pole!"

History documents the occasional human practice of solemnly taking vows of poverty, chastity, and obedience—often ignored in the face of opportunity and temptation. For example, Adam and Eve promised not to touch the forbidden fruit in the garden of Eden—figuratively and loosely translated—with a ten-foot pole. However, we all know how that story ended. Fortunately, that particular divine restriction covered forbidden fruit and did not apply to the opposite sex. There is a tremendous amount of evidence that Adam and Eve did eventually get together. And God Himself endorsed the union when He observed: "It is not good for man to live alone" (Gen. 3).

Returning our attention to that college campus of the 1930s, in spite of strict efforts to minimize and regulate contact between male and female students, the overwhelming power of youthful hormones and romantic desire eventually bridged the barriers of time and distance (the ten-foot pole). Subsequent data from that era reveal that marriage rates between college sweethearts were very high and successful. Regulations to minimize, structure, and regulate contact between male and female students were only temporary barriers. They didn't work then and don't work now. The opposite sexes still fall in love—even in old age.

## Everybody Needs Somebody Sometime

A generation later in the mid-1950s, I was a dormitory student monitor at that same college. Based upon my own observations, I can attest that the passage of time has produced a more pragmatic and tolerant policy toward campus romances. The college courtship of Henry and Annie comes to mind as a graphic example.

One afternoon I was on duty in one of the male dormitories when another student rushed up and excitedly announced that "Henry was hysterically crying in the shower room." Since one of my duties was to deal with emergencies and keep the peace, I led a small group of curious residents into a large shower room featuring twenty shower heads and a lot of humid steam. There, under a central shower, stood a wailing student. Henry was a nineteen-year-old sophomore whose most distinguishing achievement thus far was his going steady status with Annie, a young coed from a women's dormitory across campus.

We hesitated at the door to survey the scene. Other than his copious tears mingling with the pouring shower, Henry was apparently uninjured. My accompanying posse looked expectantly in my direction for some resolution. So mustering my most authoritative voice I commanded: "Henry, come out of the shower room immediately."

My fellow rescuers prepared to cover the distraught youth with towels and his clothes. However, Henry just kept bawling and refused to come out from under the shower—even when I repeated the command. My squad of supporters offered little assistance as my leadership status began to crumble. And Henry—overwhelmed by some terrible sorrow in his life—continued to weep loudly. It looked like he might founder and go under the rising flood of emotion.

With no other recourse in sight, I removed my sweater, shirt, and shoes and handed them to my companions. Then I launched into the shower room, grabbed the surprised and slippery Henry, and dragged him into the outstretched arms of my companions in the doorway. I must admit that I was furious (Henry's behavior reminded me that the meaning of the word *sophomore* is "wise fool.") I told them to get Henry dried off and dressed and hold him until I could get dry and into my clothes. Henry had finally stopped blubbering when I confronted him with the question: "Why the big performance in the shower room that worried and inconvenienced your fellow dorm residents and forced me into an impromptu shower?" We were astonished at Henry's reply: "Annie broke up with me."

I was only twenty-two years old and inexperienced in the affairs of the heart—nor had I ever before witnessed the trauma of an aborted romance. However, I instinctively realized that Henry's demonstrated sorrow was a major crisis for him that required some help. While most men seem to adopt an attitude of stoic resignation in coming to terms with such a setback, Henry could not contain his disappointment. And it occurred to me that there was a bit of information that could encourage Henry and help him get over his failed romance. So I said, "Henry, come with me for a few minutes."

I led the now contrite student to a central building with a high elevation overlooking the campus. We stood there a few minutes observing the busy scene below before I said, "Henry, what do you see?" And Henry dully replied, "I see many students on their way to classes." I then urged him to take a closer look: "Half of those college students are females—bright, attractive, unmarried young women. And what you see is just a small proportion of the many students on this campus."

Slowly, the point dawned upon Henry: "In view of all these other potential romantic interests, the loss of one girlfriend is only a small and temporary setback. There are many other fish in the sea. The quickest cure for the loss of a campus girlfriend is another girl. Good hunting,

Henry!" And Henry gained a broader and wiser perspective from that high place before descending back into the college dating game.

From that college experience with Henry, I became aware of a major guiding principle of human love and romance: Everybody needs somebody sometime. Though Henry and Annie's connection and breakup was more public and dramatic than most romantic affairs, their conflicted joy and sadness are replicated in countless couples every day. There is probably a little of Henry and Annie in all of us. We are biologically and socially preprogrammed and compelled to embark upon the thrilling and threatening, the daring and dangerous, quest for love.

## The Romantic Impulse

Let's turn our attention to more examples and expressions of romance, courtship, and the dating and mating game. Among most animal species, distinctive courtship behavior has been observed prior to mating. Consider the extraordinary displays and dances of male birds-of-paradise in New Guinea that transform themselves into beguiling spectacles to attract females. Males of other bird species rely less on physical appearance to attract females but demonstrate their romantic intentions with a serenade of lovely songs, the building of intricate nests, or a vigorous defense of territory. The initial caution and apparent reluctance of females to enter into a breeding relationship is because she obviously will be the partner that goes through pregnancy and thus will have a much greater investment in the relationship than the eager male (Barash 1982).

There is an accumulating body of evidence that human beings use some of the same tactics in attracting marriage and mating partners. Men seem to be instinctively aware that they are being evaluated and compared to other suitors by potential spouses. Culturally, they are expected to demonstrate the manly attributes necessary to sire healthy offspring and support a family. They typically respond to these expectations by competing with other potential suitors and making physical and social overtures to attractive women.

Men may fall in love more spontaneously than women and are caught up in the excitement of the chase after the alluring face and form. On the other hand, It has been suggested that the female of the human species (like her counterparts in the animal kingdom) may unconsciously be more cautious and calculating in evaluating the opportunities and choices for a romantic partner—based on the demonstrated promise and potential of the male. In short—we have an old cultural tradition that it is the man's option to make his move. And it is the female's choice to voluntarily accept or reject the would-be suitor. Currently, slowly evolving social norms have begun to modify some of these behavioral standards.

## The Music of Love

The proposition that men are generally more spontaneous, intense, and overtly romantic than women is supported by intriguing findings from a survey of musical composers and their love songs. I found that America's male troubadours are irrepressible romantics. During my lifetime, I have heard many hundreds of popular songs written and performed by love-struck men extolling the virtues and beauty of the face, hands, hair, voice, smile, personality, and character of the female objects of their affection.

To cite just a sample of countless examples, many in my generation have loved and lamented with vocalists over "Beautiful Brown Eyes," "Blue Eyes," "Dark Eyes," and "Smiling Irish Eyes." We have danced "The Tennessee Waltz" with our darlings, and bid "Goodnight, Irene" to a favorite girl. We have carried the torch for "Peg O' My Heart," "Mona Lisa," and "My Gal Sal." We have fantasized that "Some Enchanted Evening" we would look across a crowded room and spot the Girls of our dreams. After all the years, we still pine for "Sweet Adeline" and "Ruby"—who "took her love to town." We have cried with John Denver over "Annie's Song;" and we are still looking with The Texas Playboys for the "Rose of San Antonio." We cheered Nelson Eddy as he tramped across the tundra bellowing "Rose Marie, I love you," and joined Marty Robbins in the "El Paso" gunfight over Selena—the dancing girl in Rosa's cantina.

So the dominant musical pattern of lovesick Romeos is well-established. There is nothing comparable to this magnitude among female composers or performers extolling the physical or social traits of their boyfriends. (The only song complimenting the biological attributes of a man that comes to my mind is Tennessee Ernie Ford's rendition of "Big, Bad John" who heroically saved his comrades from a mine cave-in.)

The record for composing love songs goes to Stephen Foster, often known as "the father of American music." Apparently Steve was smitten by every pretty face in every lonely place he visited. In a very large proportion of his over two hundred songs he sang of "Angelina," Nelly Bly," "Cora Dean," and her sister "Lily Dean," "Annie My Own Love," "Delcy Jones," "Dolly Day," "Ellen Bayne," "Eulalie," "Fairy Bell," "Louisiana Belle," "Katy Belle," "Virginia Bell," "Gentle Lena Claire," "Molly," "Mary Dear," "Laura Lee," "My Alice Fair," "Oh Susanna!," "Jeanie with the Light Brown Hair," and many others.

Foster also sadly lamented his lost loves in "Linda Has Departed," "Lulu Is Gone," "Farewell My Love," "Come with Thy Sweet Voice Again," "Come Where My Love Lies Dreaming," and a host of others. Clearly, Stephen Foster was socially busy and compiled a remarkable record—considering that he was just thirty-seven years old when he died. Even if Foster's amorous exploits were not fully grounded in reality, his songs do reveal an incredible amount of imagination and aspiration. He truly epitomized the male role described by the King of Siam as "like a honey bee, flitting from flower to flower."

While few people have the marathon level of preoccupation with romantic love exemplified by Stephen Foster, a more modest urge to experience romantic love is natural and normal for both men and women—persisting throughout the human life course and even into old age.

## Romance at the Rest Home

Several years ago at the university where I taught, several sociology graduate students conducted an illuminating research project at a retirement and assisted living facility. The research objective was to gain insight into the lifestyle, perspective, and problems of elderly residents from the inside. An unexpected and fascinating finding was the documentation of the lifelong human propensity of romantic attraction for the opposite sex.

The research investigation was initiated when the graduate students arranged for one of their number—disguised as an elderly woman—was admitted as a new resident to the retirement center. Her disguise consisted of a scraggly, white-haired wig, old-fashioned dress and shoes, thick reading glasses, an unnatural voice, a wheelchair, and a feigned slightly disoriented demeanor. Cosmetics completed the disguise with a lined and aged countenance. Our student was so transformed in appearance and behavior that even her friends did not recognize her (Bynum 1985).

During the week that our disguised student lived in the retirement home, she observed that elderly residents did not spend all their time knitting, playing bingo, watching television, and dozing. Many residents of both sexes were socially active and several participated in banter and flirting. A few were even seen holding hands. Some women competed openly for the attention of the greatly outnumbered men with offers of conversation and cookies. Our disguised student was hit on (romantically approached) by two elderly and lonely gentlemen. One aged Lothario secretly confided that he was a visiting king in search of a princess. "When my knights arrive," he told her, "we will all go back to the castle." (His claims of royalty were obviously deceit, delusion, or dementia.)

## Old People in Love

I have chosen to close this chapter of probably my last book with the perspective of love shared by Margaret and me. Our relationship began as college sweethearts, and soon we will celebrate our sixtieth wedding anniversary. That is a long time—well over a half century—but it seems like just yesterday that we were a young couple—naively and hopefully looking into the future together. Now—after a lifetime of hard work, educational and economic struggles, travel all over the country, countless blessings, two great children and six promising grandchildren—we are battle-scarred veterans of life, and still in love.

We believe that genuine love, courtship, and marriage are sacred and enduring (1 Cor. 13). An elderly widow in our area captured our attention and admiration as she dissuaded a courtly gentleman seeking her companionship. He was attractive, affluent, pleasant, and spiritually inclined. In the course of their conversations he diplomatically pointed out that the passing of her husband a decade earlier had freed her from the marriage commitment "until death we do part." And she thoughtfully and gently replied: "I remember those words very well—pledging our love 'until death we do part.' But I am still alive and will always be in love with my husband." To that, the would-be-suitor sighed: "I have had keen competition before, but love for a dead man is a hard act to follow."

The long journey that Margaret and I have made together was only possible because we made it as a team. We have had each other to lean on and hold hands with as we crossed the demanding deserts of education, work, and careers; climbed the challenging mountains of home, family, and parenthood; and sailed the uncertain seas of failing health. Our youthful appearance and strength have long since faded. Sometimes I tell people that we have become so old and weak that together we now equal one strong person. And that combination is proving to be enough to see us through.

We are like two old trees in our Lithia Park. The gnarled oak and the tender maple have stood side by side so long that they have literally grown together. Their ancient trunks and limbs are inseparably joined and intertwined, giving them the combined strength and support to survive together the many storms of life. Those two old trees represent a living parable of a good marriage. And perhaps they perfectly illustrate the meaning of God's words when He said: *"A man shall ... cleave unto his wife and they shall become as one"* (Gen. 2:24).

## When You and I Were Young, Maggie

The dedication at the beginning of this book succinctly expresses the past, present, and future relationship of my wife and me in three poignant Latin phrases: *"Amavimus, amamus, amabimus."* Translated, these magical words mean: *"We have loved, we love, we shall love."*

Last Valentine's Day, I arranged for a local ladies quartet—The Sweet Adelines—to make a surprise visit to our home and serenade

Margaret. I had requested an old-fashioned song that seems to expresses our experience and love through the years:

> *I wandered today to the hill, Maggie*
> *To watch the scene below*
> *The creek and the rusty old mill, Maggie*
> *Where we sat in the long, long ago*
> *The green grove is gone from the hill, Maggie*
> *Where first the daisies sprung*
> *The old rusty mill is still, Maggie*
> *Since you and I were young.*
>
> *They say I am feeble with age, Maggie*
> *My steps are less sprightly than then*
> *My face is a well-written page, Maggie*
> *But time alone was the pen.*
> *They say we are aged and grey Maggie*
> *As spray by the white breakers flung*
> *But to me you're as fair as you were, Maggie*
> *When you and I were young.*
>
> *For now we are aged and grey, Maggie*
> *The trials of life nearly done*
> *Let us sing of the days that are gone, Maggie*
> *When you and I were young.*

(George W. Johnson and J.A. Butterfield 1866)

# CHAPTER TWENTY

## The Entrepreneurs

An *entrepreneur* is defined as "a person who organizes, manages, or promotes a business undertaking, product, or service—assuming the risk for the sake of the profit." As a result of this commitment, the entrepreneur generally pursues marketing and sales with enthusiasm and tenacity. It can safely be assumed that everyone, during his or her lifetime, will have encountered or been targeted by both professional and amateur entrepreneurs—or may personally have been an entrepreneur.

A slowing economy has not placed them on the list of endangered species. On the contrary, they are stimulated ever more in their use of aggressive advertising, social media, and all other marketing strategies. In just one recent week, I have been directly approached, encouraged, enticed, solicited, propositioned, and even warned of impending disasters unless I purchased more and better insurance, home alarm devices, increased my storage of food, stocked survival equipment, and moved to a mountain sanctuary. All these emergency purchase opportunities remind me of the old and accurate proverb: "Let the buyer beware!"

Even in our comfortable, secure hometown of Ashland, we are besieged and bombarded by tenacious people trying to sell us something (or anything). A few examples will illustrate the phenomena. We have so much to celebrate here in Southern Oregon. In fact, we never stop celebrating. Throughout the year, we celebrate the Shakespeare Festival, the Cheese Festival, the Film Festival, the Pear Blossom Festival, the Wine Festival (complete with barefooted college girls stomping on grapes), and the Chocolate Festival in which one hairdresser advertises a chocolate shampoo. Not to be outdone, a local masseur offers a chocolate massage to chocoholics.

On one occasion, early in our Ashland sojourn, Margaret and I attended the annual Robert Burns Memorial Festival in which an estimated eight hundred tourists join the "gathering of the clans" in a large auditorium. We observed the most ardent fans of Bobbie Burns don kilts, adopt a Scottish accent, try out the bagpipes, sing "Coming Through the Rye," and fortified with a wee bit of Scotch whiskey, partake of the traditional Scotch dish of haggis. That particular delicacy is comprised of ground oats and the lungs and heart of an animal, cooked together in a sheep's stomach, and served piping hot. ("Yummy!" or "Ugh!"— depending how loyal one is to the ancient land of the heather.)

All this community fun and frolic is a transparent sales pitch designed to separate potential patrons from their money. In addition, there is the ongoing hoopla among more naturalistic locals in promoting medicinal marijuana and organic fruits and vegetables—produced without the artificial aid of pesticides, insecticides, fertilizers, and preservatives. A few ungrateful critics have complained that in some instances, this produce is characterized by inferior size, color, and taste—and supplemented by the presence of larva and worms.

Our entrepreneurial society also offers a wide variety of more exotic and mystical services such as a storefront fortune-teller who—for a fee— will forecast the occupational, matrimonial, and monetary futures of her clients. Every time I drive past our fortune-teller's humble place of business, I wonder why her gifted ability to predict the future has not made her a winner at the Grants Pass horse races or in the statewide lottery.

## The Bynum Backache

Several years ago I received an unexpected injury. My father was a building contractor, and ever since I was fifteen years old, I easily lifted the tongue of his utility trailer and hitched it to a pickup truck for hauling various building materials. In later years I inherited that old utility trailer and have continued to use it for occasional trips to the municipal dump. On my last routine hookup of the trailer, I was amazed to discover that somehow—between my adolescent age of fifteen years and my present age of eighty plus years—that trailer has gained an immense amount of weight. In lifting the tongue to the truck hitch, I felt a sudden and surprising pain in my lower back. The result was a chronic backache. After investing considerable money in the services of a chiropractor and a physical therapist without much relief, I met with a surgeon who specializes in backaches. As he outlined the graphic details of his proposed surgery, my back condition miraculously seemed less critical than I had earlier thought. I adopted a position of wait and see what develops.

## An Acupuncture Experience

As my nagging backache persisted, I finally decided to visit a local oriental-themed acupuncture clinic set up at the former site of a bankrupt physical fitness gym. I knew nothing about the acupuncture treatment other than the skin is penetrated with narrow needles that are then manipulated manually or by electrical stimulation. Theoretically, this process is supposed to correct systemic imbalances and relieve pain related to many physical ailments. The process itself sounded painful but was worth the risk if it provided relief from my aching back.

I arrived at Madam Butterfly's acupuncture clinic where I was greeted by an inscrutable, diminutive woman wearing a flowing kimono, wooden sandals, and several layers of cosmetics. Butterfly registered my name, collected an up-front fee of twenty dollars, and asked the nature of my physical or emotional problem. She then ushered me into a large, dimly lit room and turned me over to a similarly-dressed technician identified as Lotus Blossom. They solemnly bowed to me and to each other before assigning me a seat in a large recliner.

As my eyes adjusted to the subdued lighting, I noticed six or seven other patrons silently reclining in similar chairs. All of them had long shiny needles sticking in their hands, ear lobes, and other body parts. I had a moment of anxiety when I observed one gentleman with a needle embedded in his face. If he was trying to get attention it certainly worked! The sound of silence was oppressive—only interrupted by unusual music featuring chimes and bells playing in the background. The room was also filled with the aroma of burning incense. Just as I began to choke, Lotus Blossom reappeared with a tray of needles and went to work on my backache.

Lotus deftly began inserting needles in my hands, arms, and body until I began to look like I had encountered an angry porcupine. It occurred to me that the secret of acupuncture may be in replacing painful ailments with something new to think about. I wished I had listed fear and hysteria among my symptoms to Madam Butterfly. Surprisingly, the needles—while intimidating—seemed almost painless and bloodless. (I had heard that shock can do that too!) Lotus left me alone to meditate and contemplate the healing needles and my surroundings. Madam Butterfly retired to a balcony position overlooking the proceedings.

In about ten minutes, my tranquility began to unravel when the large, daggerlike needle in my side began to hurt. Sneaking a peek, I was disturbed to see a dark and spreading bruise just below the rib cage (probably a mild hematoma from a leaking blood vessel just under the surface of the skin). When my new bruise approached the size of a dollar bill, I sounded the alarm: first with low and polite moans and groans. Attracting no response, I followed with a more affective howl (learned from *The Call of the Wild* by Jack London).

When the other, more comatose patients began to stir, Lotus rushed to my side, pursing her lips for silence. As I continued to indicate stress, Madam Butterfly descended from her lofty perch like an irritated dragonfly and accused me of disrupting the ambience and healing atmosphere in the treatment room. My outcry finally ended when they removed my needles, and I was asked to leave. When I forfeited my entrance fee I again raised my voice in protest—hoping she might remember that the United States has become a friend of Japan since World War II. My complaint was to no avail.

I decided to tough out my backache at home with heat applications and mild exercises prescribed by my physical therapist. Slowly—over a period of six weeks—the pain and stiffness began to diminish. Other than learning a few basic phrases in Japanese (some of which I suspect may be profanity), I gained nothing from my acupuncture adventure. This is not to deny that acupuncture treatments may benefit some patients. I am confident that Madam Butterfly and Lotus Blossom could cite many instances of physical relief derived from acupuncture therapy. They would argue that I had leaned on reason more than faith—that I was focused more on the needle than my need. And I would probably agree with that assessment.

~~

## Age-Specific Entrepreneurship

The most recent US Census data confirms the trend of an aging American population. That is, lower birth rates and longer life spans have combined to dramatically increase the average age in our society. Correlated with this demographic phenomenon has been the emergence of the death and dying industry and an army of entrepreneurs intent on exploiting the commercial opportunities available through senior citizens. Their objective is to separate elderly people from their money.

Ever since my wife and I entered the seventieth year of our life courses, we have been contacted by an increasing number of companies or their agents boldly targeting our diminishing physical, mental, and social viability, and urging us to make important economic decisions under their fraternal guidance. Here are just a few such opportunities that have come our way:

Margaret and I first suspected that someone besides God was keeping score of our longevity past the biblical three score and ten years. There has been a tremendous increase in requests for contributions from all of the schools we attended as students or served as faculty members. For example, the alumni journals and newsletters never remind us of our student struggles to pay tuition, endure the academic grind, and survive the political and social competition. Rather, the communications from some of our alma maters mainly focus on the warm and fuzzy memories of old friendships and good times on *"ye olde campus"* as a sentimental appeal for financial support.

Then one day someone in a university endowment office took note of our advancing ages and made some assumptions regarding the quality and quantity of our resources and our enduring love for the school. Soon we began receiving suggestions that we make a final and sizeable endowment to help fund campus improvements and worthy students. It's nice to be noticed and remembered—but not in the context of a pending obituary.

Similar appeals from charitable and religious organizations urge us to plan *now* to leave a significant contribution as our legacy to the churches and causes that have been the inspirational guides throughout our lives. It bothers us a bit to hear ourselves referred to in the past tense. And many of the educational, welfare, and religious institutions generously offer to prepare our last will and testament—at no cost for this legal service—but in the hope of favorable mention in the disposition of our worldly goods.

The funeral industry has also been quick to remind us that we were *getting on in years* and that as merchants of death, our local funeral and cemetery directors are ready and willing (yes—even eager) to offer their professional assistance in planning our last rites. Their favorite and highly recommended plan is the prepaid funeral in which for a bargain price, we can relax and "leave the details to them."

The showroom for displaying coffins or caskets, urns for ashes, and other funeral props and furnishings that we visited was even larger than the chapel. Casket styles and prices begin with the ornate and expensive top-of-the line models for those family survivors who—according to a mortuary representative—"realize that their departed loved one deserves only the best." This perspective recalls the ancient Norse custom of a thousand years ago when Eric the Red, Leif Erikson, and other fallen warriors and explorers qualified for the Viking funeral. After prolonged feasting and chanting on the seashore by the kinsmen and community, the corpse would be entombed in a traditional, dragon-headed long boat, set afire, and launched into a fiord for a last voyage to Valhalla.

In modern times, a deceased person who is affluent and/or famous may also be honored with extravagant funeral symbols and rituals as if he or she is going to a royal entombment in an Egyptian pyramid. On a lesser scale, an occasional and eccentric luminary has flaunted personal wealth by requesting burial in his Cadillac. Contrary to the old adage, he is trying to take it with him.

From these expensive funeral displays, the lineup of caskets is economically downhill—all the way to the proverbial pine box special for realistic families of modest means. There is even a quaint burial container made of biodegradable, woven reeds for those with a naturalistic philosophy of death and burial.

Glossy, full-color advertisements of other funeral options continue to fill our mailbox. Cremation has become a more popular mode of departure—especially compared to the much more expensive coffins and cemetery burial plots. Practical families can avoid cemetery burial expenses by retaining the ashes of a loved one at home. A mortician reported that some people find comfort in the presence of the ashes—perhaps displayed in a funerary urn on the fireplace mantle or in a backyard flower garden.

Other possibilities include a burial at sea, or having the ashes of a loved one sprinkled from an airplane (with appropriate permissions) over mountains, forests, deserts, or a favorite golf course. One creative entrepreneur has envisioned the future possibility of rocketing human remains or ashes into outer space for eternal orbit. This may be the best plan for getting closer to heaven for some less hopeful but more affluent deceased.

For those very wealthy individuals who refuse an irretrievable surrender of their mortal remains to the grave, the Kryonics Institute in Michigan will store a dead body in a deep freeze condition. The current base price for this preparation and storage service is just $108,000. At a later time, after new scientific miracles of healing and restoration have been developed, the plan calls for the body to be thawed, revived, and cured of the disease that originally caused the subject's demise—all for additional fees. Among others, the remains of Ted Williams—the baseball legend—are purportedly frozen in anticipation of a future cure and resurrection.

When Margaret and I approached our eightieth birthdays, we noticed an abrupt loss of interest in us by life insurance companies. However, we did see a great increase in the entrepreneurs of death and dying—circling like vultures with strategies to tap into our life savings and other resources. We have been repeatedly approached with opportunities to donate our home, cars, stock, savings bonds, and life insurance policies to worthy causes.

There are others who have suggested donating our bodies for medical research. Our son, a physician—who had some experience with cadavers in medical school—has indignantly rejected this notion for disposing of his parents' bodies. And the futuristic, science-fiction Soylent Green solution for processing dead human bodies into tasteless but nutritious biscuits for a starving, overpopulated world still shows little promise of public acceptance.

We have also been asked to consider a plan to harvest our organs for transplanting in the injured bodies of younger clients. This is much more than an occasional one-pint blood donation through the Red Cross. They want our kidneys, eye corneas, lungs, and perhaps a bit of bone marrow and skin—hopefully and immediately after we die. And just a few months ago, an insensitive young salesman sat in our living room and gave an enthusiastic sales pitch to videotape an interview with us to leave behind for the family after our passing. He emphasized that his company has a deadline on the offer. Noting my advanced age, he remarked: "Age eighty is a nice full life," to which I responded: *"Not if your seventy-nine years old."*

As he kept repeating the idea of our passing, I finally turned to Margaret—who keeps a written record of all our upcoming appointments—and asked: "Do we have any appointments scheduled for our passing?" And she replied: "Yes, we have. The contract is written in the Scriptures: 'It is appointed unto man once to die and after that the judgment'" (Heb. 9:27). At that, I reached a decision for the eager young salesman of video interviews with the elderly: "We will pass on your proposition because we already have a contract with the Lord. He maintains a complete record of our lives, numbers our days, and offers a better legacy and future than you can. So we will plan our final interview and exit with Him."

～

Many years ago, Margaret and I committed our souls and eternal futures to our heavenly Father who has given us long life and abundant blessings. We are confident and secure in that spiritual decision. We also believe that we have the responsibility to make reasonable plans for the final disposition and distribution of our earthly bodies and accumulated estate. It would be foolhardy to indefinitely postpone making some fundamental decisions regarding these important matters—rather than leaving them to others without a clear understanding of our primary wishes and preferences.

With this in mind, I dare not close this chapter without advising my readers to seek the wise, confidential, and independent counsel of two or three faithful friends, a trusted minister or spiritual advisor, and a competent attorney—all of whom should care about you and none of whom have any personal interest or involvement in your estate. Then, privately and quietly, you and your spouse should make the necessary, unhurried, and unpressured decisions regarding the preparation and explicit content of your last will and testament.

# EPILOGUE
# AN OPEN LETTER: WELCOME
# TO THE FUTURE

**Dear Reader—**

Thank you for reading my book. You were in my mind when *Retirement Reorientation* was written. Having experienced the stresses and adjustments associated with my own retirement, I wanted to share my story with you and other individuals anticipating or experiencing the same transition.

In these pages you were introduced to Woody, Miss Twomley, the Southpaw, Lotus Blossom, Father Time, Fern, Lonesome John, Cousin Cleo, Senator Bulartis, the Hometown Heroes, Cowboy Mac, Jack and Margaret—the elderly couple who escorted you through the narrative—and many others. Perhaps old memories of people in your own unfolding life story were resurrected. Maybe some of the book characters are reflected in the past history and experience of the one looking back as you gaze into the mirror. My objective has been to offer some helpful insights (seasoned with a bit of humor) regarding some of the issues many of us face as we entire retirement.

You are fortunate and blessed to have come this far on your life journey. My hope and wish for you is that from this vantage point, you will look to the future as an unending adventure—filled with enriching experiences and interesting people! May God be your friend and guide!

Sincerely,
Jack Bynum

"Grow old along with me!
The best is yet to be,
The last of life, for which the first was made:
Our times are in His hand
Who saith "A whole I planned,
Youth shows but half; trust God: see all, nor be afraid!"

[From *Rabbi Ben Ezra* by Robert Browning (1812–1889)]

# REFERENCES

## Introduction

Bynum, Jack. *Once Upon a Time*. Ashland, OR: Rogue Valley Research and Publications, 2006.

## Chapter One

Ardrey, Robert. *The Territorial Imperative*. New York, NY: Atheneum Publishers, 1966.

*Gilkyson, Terry. The Cry of the Wild Goose*. 1950.

Lorenz, Konrad. *The Foundations of Ethnology*. New York, NY: Springer Publishing Co., 1981.

## Chapter Two

Associated Press. "Homeless Man Arrested in Fire that Destroyed Eleven Homes in Ashland." August 25, 2010.

Associated Press. "Naked Lady Plans to be in Ashland Parade; Officials Object." June 17, 2008.

Donoghue, Daniel. *Lady Godiva: A Literary History of the Legend*. Oxford, UK: Blackwell Publishing, LTD, 2002.

Guzik, Hannah. "What Do We Do with John Thiry?" *The Mail Tribune* January 20, 2011.

Plain, Robert. "Ashland City Council Agrees to get Therapy." *The Mail Tribune* September 7, 2007.

Specht, Sanne. "Oak Knoll Fire Suspect Jailed for Throwing Rocks at Children." *The Tidings* July 29, 2011.

## Chapter Four

Fayobserver. "Live Wire: Oleander Bushes are Pretty, but Poisonous." Wikipedia: accessed in April 2013.

Weber, Max. *The Protestant Ethic and the Spirit of Capitalism*. New York, NY: Scribner, 1958.

## Chapter Five

Capp, Al. (1909–1979). American cartoonist and humorist, best known for his satirical comic strip "Lil' Abner" (1934–1977) who was the fictitious, central character in the rustic community of Dogpatch.

## Chapter Seven

Durkheim, Emile. *The Division of Labor in Society*. New York, NY: Simon and Schuster, 1997.

Shakespeare, William. *All's Well that Ends Well. The Complete Works of William Shakespeare*. New York, NY: Barnes & Noble Publishers, 1994.

## Chapter Eight

Bynum, Jack. *The Dream Catchers*. Bloomington, IN: WestBow Press, 2011.

Thompson, William and Joseph Hickey. *Society in Focus* (3rd Edition). New York, NY: Addison, Wesley, and Longman, Inc. 1999.

## Chapter Nine

Bynum, Jack. *The Dream Catchers*. Bloomington, IN: WestBow Press, 2011.

Stonequist, Everett. *The Marginal Man*. New York, NY: Charles Scribner's Sons, 1937.

## Chapter Ten

DeKay, James and Sandy Huffaker. *The World's Greatest Left-Handers*. New York, NY: M. Evans and Company, Inc., 1985.

Rutledge, Leigh and Richard Donley. *The Left-Hander's Guide to Life*. New York, NY: Penguin Books USA, Inc., 1992.

Uecker, Bob and Mickey Herskowitz. *The Catcher in the Wry*. New York, NY: G.P. Putnam's Sons, 1982.

Wikipedia. "Handedness." Derived on November 21, 2012.

## Chapter Eleven

Ditzel, Peter. "Are Christians to Greet Each Other with a Holy Kiss?" *Wordofhisgrace.org, 2010*. Accessed from Wikipedia, July 27, 2014.

Friedman, Hershey H. and Bernard H. Stern. "Humor in the Hebrew Bible." *Humor: International Journal of Human Research*. Vol. 13:3. September 2000. Pp. 258–285.

Martin, James. *Between Heaven and Mirth: Why Joy, Humor, and Laughter are at the Heart of the Spiritual Life*. New York, NY: HarperOne, 2011.

McGhee, Paul E. "Laughter is the Best Medicine: The Health Benefits of Humor and Laughter." —Helpguide.org, Accessed May 20, 2013.

Reardon, Johannah. "Does God Have a Sense of Humor?" *Christianity Today*. November 9, 2010. Pg. 24–28.

## Chapter Thirteen

Bynum, Jack. *Once Upon a Time*. Ashland, Oregon: Rogue Valley Research and Publishing, 2006.

White, E.G. *The Ministry of Healing*. Mountain View, CA: Pacific Press, 1905.

## Chapter Fourteen

Miller, Frederick P., Agnes F. Vandome, and John McBrewster. *Horsepower*. Beau Bassin, Mauritius: Alphascript Publishing, 2009.

Shakespeare, William. Play: *Richard III The Complete Works of William Shakespeare*. New York, NY: Barnes & Noble Publishers, 1994.

## Chapter Sixteen

Rosamund, M.J., k.e. Walker and r. Montague. *Stonehenge in its Landscape: 20th Century*
Excavations. London: English Heritage Archaeological Report 10, 1995.
Work, Henry Clay. *My Grandfather's Clock*. 1876.

## Chapter Seventeen

Artist Recreation. "The Victory over New Jersey in the Hero Sandwich Wars." 2011. Derived from Wikipedia, September 5, 2013.
Cervantes, Miguel. *Don Quixote de la Mancha*. New York, NY: Random House Publishing Group: 2000.
Rice, Tim and Andrew Lloyd Weber. *Jesus Christ Superstar*. First staging on Broadway, New York City, 1971.
*Webster's New World Basic Dictionary of American English*. Cleveland, OH: Wiley Publishing, Inc., 1998.

## Chapter Eighteen

Bynum, Jack and Leo Downing. "Military Service: Alternative to Incarceration." Free Inquiry in *Creative Sociology* 9, num. 1 (May 1981).

## Chapter Nineteen

Barish, David P. *Sociobiology and Behavior* (2nd edition). New York, NY: Elsevier Science Publishers, 1982, pp. 263–267.
Bynum, Jack E. *Applied Sociology* (2nd edition). Acton, MA: Copley Publishing Group, 1985.
Utt, Walter. *A Mountain, A Pickax, A College* (3rd edition). Angwin, CA: Pacific Union College Press,1996.